W9-ASA-816

PUBLISHED ON THE
LOUIS STERN MEMORIAL FUND

Images or Shadows

of

Divine Things

by

Jonathan Edwards

Edited by PERRY MILLER

ST. JOSEPH'S UNIVERSITY STX

BL210.E3 1977
Images or shadows of divine things /

3 9353 00068 8737

178036

BL
210
.E3
1977

GREENWOOD PRESS, PUBLISHERS
WESTPORT, CONNECTICUT

Library of Congress Cataloging in Publication Data

Edwards, Jonathan, 1703-1758.
    Images or shadows of divine things.

    Reprint of the ed. published by Yale University
Press, New Haven.
    Includes bibliographical references.
    1. Analogy (Religion) 2. Typology (Theology)
I. Title.
BL210.E3 1977   230'.5'8   73-8157
ISBN 0-8371-6952-6

COPYRIGHT, 1948, BY YALE UNIVERSITY PRESS

All rights reserved. This book may not be
reproduced, in whole or in part, in any form
(except by reviewers for the public press),
without written permission from the publishers.

Originally published in 1948 by Yale University Press,
New Haven
Reprinted with the permission of Yale University
Press

Reprinted in 1977 by Greenwood Press, Inc.
51 Riverside Avenue, Westport, CT 06880

Library of Congress catalog card number 73-8157
ISBN 0-8371-6952-6

Printed in the United States of America

10 9 8 7 6 5 4 3 2

For

RALPH BARTON PERRY

FOREWORD

This edition of Edwards' manuscript endeavors to fulfill, as far as possible, the author's intention. Since Edwards never designed it for publication, at least in its present form, and jotted down his thoughts in the heat of the moment, preparation of the manuscript has demanded certain modifications which, it is hoped, will make it readable by modern standards and yet do no violence to the original. The spelling and syntax are Edwards', but the punctuation is almost entirely supplied; his abbreviations and contractions have been expanded. His casual capitalizations have been regularized. Where he refers to passages in other manuscripts, clearly intending them to be incorporated in this, the designated sections have been added.

My thanks are due to the Yale University Library for making available the manuscripts and for granting permission to publish them. I am indebted to the Library of the Andover-Newton Theological Seminary for permitting me to use the Edwards transcripts, without which no student of Edwards can cope with his difficult script. I have profited from conversation about typology, as well as about other topics, with Prof. Werner Jaeger. It is a pleasure to record that the work added one more to a long series of debts to Harriett and Cornelius Osgood. Invaluable assistance was freely given by Prof. Leonard W. Labaree, and Prof. Norman Holmes Pearson stands in the relation of a godfather to the enterprise. Preparation of the edition was the work both of the nominal editor and of Elizabeth Williams Miller.

PERRY MILLER

Harvard University,
  August 15, 1947

CONTENTS

INTRODUCTION

"A cipher has a double meaning, one clear, and one in which it is said that the meaning is hidden."

PASCAL, *Pensées*, 676.

I. TROPES AND TYPES

AMONG the manuscripts of Jonathan Edwards, which after many vicissitudes came to rest in the Library of Yale University, is a homemade, hand-stitched folio to which Edwards gave various titles: "The Images of Divine Things," "The Shadows of Divine Things," "The Book of Nature and Common Providence," "The Language and Lessons of Nature." It contains 212 numbered entries; the handwriting indicates that the notations were made, with different pens and inks, throughout his life. Many of them were put down in haste and are only the seeds of ideas; in his crowded and intense life he had little time to develop them.

Certainly the manuscript in its surviving form was never intended for publication. From his college days Edwards dreamed of writing a systematic "Rational Account of the Main Doctrines of the Christian Religion Attempted," in which he proposed "to show how all arts and sciences, the more they are perfected, the more they issue in divinity, and coincide with it, and appear to be as parts of it." [1] The first sketches for this project are the fragments we know as "Notes on the Mind" and "Notes on Science," written while he was an undergraduate at Yale College between 1716 and 1720, not published until 1830; on them Edwards' fame as a metaphysician largely rests. It is less well known that throughout his life he kept a journal, provisionally entitled "Miscellanies," into which he poured his best thought and out of which he intended to construct the monumental "Account." The manuscript of "Images" was kept separately, and with care. It was to be a part, an essential part, of the "Account," but he never found time to make it more than a series of jottings.

The manuscript consists, then, of 212 notes for a work in progress. Previous scholars have remarked its existence, but it has appeared too fragmentary to excite serious consideration. It must be read, of course, in the light of Edwards' ultimate ambition, which was only adumbrated in the youthful "Notes" and lies still unrealized in the almost undecipherable "Miscellanies." Yet the "Images," if studied sympathetically, do form a theme which is implied, sometimes deliberately veiled, in the published works. (His unpublished sermons are often more explicit on this topic than those in print; his editors never understood him and omitted passages in which he expounded this puzzling concept.) In short, these rough notes are the draft of an idea fundamental to Edwards' thinking. Crude and abrupt, they are in effect a spiritual autobiography. The manuscript lets us see his mind at work, fashioning and refining an idea, repeating and deepening it, from the first glimpses through successive moments of illumination to the last ecstatic cry when the words were thrown on the paper in an exclamation that defies the restraints of prose. The theme of the "Images" carries us to the very heart of Edwards' system.

At first sight the manuscript seems to be nothing but a catalogue of morals to be read into natural phenomena by a pious, though to our taste naïve, mind. It seems to be a collection of what the previous century had called "emblems," remarkable merely for their rather rigid precision. English literature in the golden age of religious expression had been rich in imagery. In the seventeenth century a habit of reading sermons in stone was universal, as indeed it had been for many Christian centuries; metaphysical poets had found exemplification of religious truths in the most unlikely occurrences, and nature was pressed into the service of the highest mysteries by Jacobean and Carolinian essayists and philosophers as well as divines. The brooding tenderness of Jeremy Taylor, finding illustrations of spiritual laws in the commonest objects of experience, created those sustained similes that are a glory of English prose:

But so have I seen a rose newly springing from the clefts of its hood, and at first it was fair as the morning, and full with the dew of heaven as a lamb's fleece; but when a ruder breath had forced open its virgin modesty, and dismantled its too youthful and unripe retirements, it began to put on darkness, and to decline to softness and the symptoms of a sickly age; it bowed the head, and broke its stalk, and at night having lost some of its leaves and all its beauty, it fell into the portion of weeds and outworn faces.[2]

Even Anglican devotional writers were read in New England, and the habit of finding symbols of the abstract in the concrete was a part of the literary tradition from the days of the first masters, Thomas Hooker, John Cotton, and Thomas Shepard.

In the Puritan as opposed to the Anglican tradition, there was an articulated doctrine governing the use of emblems and allegories. Puritanism was a protest not only against the polity of the Church of England but also against its esthetic, against ritual and ornamentation in the worship and elegance in the sermon. Puritanism raised the standard of the "plain style." So, while Puritans might read Jeremy Taylor and approve his piety as far as it could be separated from his polity, they distrusted his poetry. To find in the rose a symbol of the predicament of sinful man was allowable, but so to dwell upon its beauty that the rose became more moving than the predicament, or that the music of the words diverted attention from the thematic assertion, was to lose the spiritual in the corporeal. It was, said the Puritan, to make an idol out of nature, and that was a sin. It was to forget the doctrine of divine providence. Everything in experience was specifically and continuously ordered by God; the rising of the sun, the blowing of the wind, the very breathing of the lungs, were all, like the decay of the rose, immediate acts of God, ordained for good and sufficient reasons. Events might conform to "laws" of nature, but only because those were God's "usual" methods of acting. To the Puritan, phenomena had significance because they were intentional. In causing this particular rose to be blasted on precisely such and such an evening, God had a purpose. The duty of man was to observe the event and to find out the purpose; most decidedly, it was not to give way to an emotion, whether of admiration or terror, excited by the appearance of things.

By temperament and by deliberate intention the Puritan was less of an "imagist" than the Anglican and more of an "allegorist." He was not insensible to beauty or sublimity, but in the face of every experience he was obliged to ask himself, What does this signify? What is God saying to me at this moment? And for furnishing significances, any event or object would do as well as any other, a pot or a pan, a rose or a lark—whatever made the meaning clearer was the better. The result in Puritan writing was an insistent literalness that sometimes, to our eyes, verges on the pedantic, but at its best, as in John Bunyan, achieves a realism that is at the same time an implicit symbolism, because the plain statement of fact vibrates with spiritual overtones. The concreteness of *Pilgrim's Progress* and *Mr. Badman,* where a great wealth of observation is employed directly for thematic assertion, is the supreme achievement of this Puritan esthetic.

Puritan use of the tropes and the figures of rhetoric was further delimited by an important sociological consideration. Puritan literature was ac'.lressed to the people, the common people, and therefore was always dominated by a principle of utility. A sermon or a tract was to be, God willing, a "means of grace." As the words of a preacher were striking the ears of listeners, God was conveying His grace to them; as the arguments of the writer were persuading the minds of readers, God was working their conversion. The similes of Puritan literature therefore had to be plain, even homely. The masses could not be affected by images taken from the world of gentlemen and scholars, from cultivated gardens full of roses or sciences full of curiosities. A trope for the trope's sake was blasphemy, and an illustration that went over the heads of the congregation was a sin against the Holy Ghost. The Puritan image had to be clearly applicable to the proposition, and it had to be drawn from a range of experience familiar to ordinary men. Ordinary men in both Englands were mostly farmers or artisans; hence a comparison involving the plowing of a field or the making of a clock was worth more than a thousand that poetized the rose. The Puritan stylist studiously held his fancy in check, sought his metaphors and similes in the commonplace, and remorselessly extracted the last ounce of meaning by a direct translation of the trope into moral so that nothing would be left to the imagination of the reader. He sought communication, not expression. The masterpieces of New England literature, the writers like Hooker and Shepard whom Jonathan Edwards revered and whose spiritual successor he accounted himself, set the pattern. Hooker expounded the relation of God to an erring mortal in an image that may be cited as the essence of the Puritan stylistic ideal:

Looke as it is with a childe that travels to a Faire with his father, or goeth into a crowd, his eye is alwayes upon his father; he bids him doe not gaze about and lose mee, the child is carefull to keep his father within sight and view, and then if hee bee weake and weary, his father can take him by the hand, and lead him, or take him into his arms and carry him; or if there be anything hee wants, or would have, his father can buy it for him, bestow it upon him; but if the childe bee carelesse and gazeth about this thing and that thing, and never lookes after his father; hee is gone one way, and his father another, he cannot tell where to finde him: whose fault is it now? it is not because hee could not keepe within the view of him, but because he out of carelessnesse lost the sight of his father.[3]

This was the tradition already at hand, already venerable, when Jonathan Edwards, the most sensitive stylist in American Puritanism, began to express the thoughts within him.

However, once Edwards did begin, in the privacy of his study, to put down his thoughts and to formulate his sermons, he found that his task was not only to perpetuate the manners of the founders, it was also to reform those of his contemporaries. To his unclouded vision it was apparent that the Puritan spirit in New England had become decadent, and in its decline the forms of expression, essential to the very being of a Puritan society, had become insidiously corrupted. He was faced with the realization of a crisis which was no less grave because he alone perceived it. The roots of the crisis go far back into the history of Christianity. From Apostolic times true believers had found the employment of even the simplest tropes of rhetoric challenged by another method of conceiving language that advanced pretensions to absolute authority, the method generally known as "typology." Typology was a system of interpreting the rhetoric of the Bible, and because it supposedly had the sanction of revelation, it could claim precedence over merely human rhetoric, and sometimes went so far as to condemn all other rhetoric entirely. Typology goes back at least as far as Origen and fourth-century Alexandria, but it had suffered varying fortunes through the Christian era. The basis of the science was an assumption that the Old Testament should be expounded not so much as a body of doctrine but as a series of prophetical adumbrations of Christ. In all its many formulations, typology held that particular events in biblical history were "types" or direct rehearsals of the ultimate act, the "antitype." Thus Jonah's three days in the belly of the whale were a type of the burial of Christ. Types were not allegories or emblems or fictitious narratives, the spirit of which might be that of Christ, but they were preliminary, factual prefigurations of what Christ finally did. Typology repeatedly gave rise to a host of extravagances, but even at its most fantastic it strove to distinguish between the type, which was true, and the trope, which was merely invention and therefore suspect. In the type there must be evidence of the one eternal intention; in the trope there can be evidence only of the intention of one writer. The type exists in history and its meaning is factual; as Pascal, to whom typology was precious, put it, "The type has been made according to the truth, and the truth has been recognized according to the type." [4] By contrast, the allegory, the simile, and the metaphor have been made according to the fancy of men, and they mean whatever the brain of the begetter is pleased they should mean. In the type there is a rigorous correspondence, which is not a

chance resemblance, between the representation and the antitype; in the trope there is correspondence only between the thing
and the associations it happens to excite in the impressionable but
treacherous senses of men. In cultures where the Bible, with all
its figurative language, is taken seriously as the word of God,
there exists a latent conflict between the rhetoric of heaven and
of earth, which is sometimes manifested as a conflict, or perhaps as
a confusion, between the type and the trope.

The conflict would never have become severe had typologists
confined their method to the Bible alone, but by the nature of
their enterprise and by the example of Scripture they had been
again and again obliged to subject more than the Bible to their
rules of interpretation. The Old Testament is history; for Christianity it was *the* history. The fascination which typology exerted
on great minds in many centuries, from Origen to Pascal, a
fascination which modern criticism comparative religion, and
philosophy of history have dispelled, was its promise of deliver-
ing a unified meaning for history. If the types could be finally
deciphered, history would be no longer a haphazard series of
events but the steady accomplishment of a purpose. Furthermore, history was enacted in nature. Many scriptural events in-
volved natural phenomena, which therefore must have their
meanings no less than the actions they had framed. The waters
of Babylon were as typical as the Babylonian captivity. And
water, along with the sun and the moon, the stars and the trees,
is still with us. Do not all these things, therefore, continue to
be types? By an unavoidable compulsion, typology was forced to
seek for a unity greater than that of the Bible, a unity of history,
nature, and theology. Could this ever be achieved, it would indeed be the supreme "Rational Account." The possibility of this
achievement intrigued the most widely ranging minds of many
ages.

Throughout these ages there was also, as has often been re-
marked, a close connection between typology and Christian art.
The first ministers of New England, most of whom studied at
Cambridge, may have recollected, even in the wilderness, the

windows of King's College. They had no intention of erecting such sensuous memorials in their college in Massachusetts (any more than certain of their grandchildren ever intended to set up cathedral architecture in their college in Connecticut), but they worked out a Puritan equivalent in their sermons on scriptural types. Congregations in frontier settlements could be more thrilled by learning that the congregation of Israel, exiled from Egypt into the wilderness in the form of army with banners, was a type of the church, and that consequently they themselves were the antitype, than the sons of English gentry, dissipating their time at the university, would ever be edified by the windows at King's. Yet, at the moment New England was settled, Puritan divines were agreed that typology was a rather subordinate department of theology. The reason was that they were still close enough to the Reformation to share in Luther and Calvin's violent rejection of the typology of the scholastics. The late Middle Ages had found the decoding of types so congenial that they had turned interpretation of the Bible into a fabulous game. By the fifteenth century scholastic nominalists had worked out a nine-fold scheme which was so complicated that even they could not keep the levels distinct; to the eyes of the reformers the mixture of literal, grammatical, allegorical, moral, anagogical, tropical readings by which the types were supposedly being expounded had become something far more impious than anything a pagan rhetorician had ever imagined. The reformers rescued the Bible from this thicket of typology with a round declaration that it contained only one simple, plain teaching. Hence the Puritans were still suspicious of typology. They would preach that Joseph's descent into the pit was a type of the burial of Christ, but they stayed on the safe ground of such obvious parallels and did not press analogies too far. They were mainly concerned with extracting from the Bible not types but sound doctrine. They were happy when expounding Moses and Aaron as types of church and state, not for the metaphysical charms of the conception but because it gave an occasion for advancing the Puritan social polemic.[5]

In general, however, they were clear that a type was not the same thing as a trope. Joseph in the pit might be a prophecy of Christ, whereas every child lost at a fair was not the factual counterpart of an erring saint but a phenomenon which Hooker and his people had observed many times, and which, therefore, he could legitimately employ to illustrate his point. The simile had validity only because Hooker happened to think of it, and his people would understand it. So anything in nature or in history might serve as a rhetorical figure if it thereby helped to make a doctrine comprehensible. The creative imagination of the Puritan preacher was free, within the limits of the plain style, to employ such tropes as he could. The Puritans were practical men who took their theory as dogma so that they could get on with their business, which was reforming society, dethroning a King, and settling New England. It did not occur to them that the line between the trope and the type needed any further demarcation, or that as long as the rules of the plain style held sway there was any possibility of simple metaphors being so abused that to the greatest intellect among their descendants the pious tropes would appear as much a nuisance to true piety as the scholastic types had seemed to the reformers.

II. THE LUXURIANCE OF THE TROPES

In the course of a century of incessant preaching and writing, Puritan spokesmen found themselves, to their bewilderment, the victims of certain underlying contradictions in their philosophy of expression. They found, by sad experience, that biblical images were not always so easily convertible into doctrines as had been supposed. The conceptions of the Bible are sometimes richly rhetorical: all theologians have been uncomfortable with "The Song of Solomon," but even the Psalms and the prophets occasionally soar to heights which, by the strict standards of the plain style, are a bit excessive. No wonder men like Lancelot Andrewes and Jeremy Taylor, undisciplined by the Puritan esthetic, were seduced. The Puritans had assumed that they were proof against such blandishments because of their steady devotion to the principle of literal interpretation. They could not imagine that the word of God ever indulged in verbal exuberance for exuberance's sake; therefore the tropes of the Bible were always to be unscrambled, as though they constituted some esoteric code, into plain declarative sentences. As Puritans read the Apostle Paul, he taught them how to go about it: "For the invisible things of him since the creation of the world are clearly seen, being perceived through the things that are made." The metaphors and hyperboles of the Old Testament, as well as the bizarre rites of the Mosaic law, had been among the things that were made. They therefore were to be "opened," and the doctrines, which were "invisible," extracted from them, like the meat from a nut. The Puritan mind shows itself at perhaps its most limited when it takes "Suffer little children to come unto me" as meaning only a condemnation of antipaedobaptists. It should be said that the literalizing habit did not mean that Puritans were always deaf to the deeper tone of the Bible; the mind of Samuel Sewall moved with unself-conscious ease from feeding his chickens to the thought of Christ feeding the saints with spiritual comforts, and though to our taste the way in which Puritans like Sewall appropriated the figurative language into their daily discourse seems incongruous, it often had the effect not of prostituting the figure but of transfiguring the conversation. Still, the fact remains that a century of experience was forcing even Puritans to recognize that a great many biblical metaphors were so highly metaphorical, so purely imaginative, that they could be decoded into a variety of meanings, some of which were not those of the *Westminster Confession*. By the rhetorical doctrine, any event or object in nature might be used to illustrate any number of propositions; it began to look as though biblical illustrations might likewise yield up any number of doctrines to as many readers. Not only did Quakers and Baptists find unorthodox meanings, but sound theologians could not agree on many essential passages. And then, by the beginning of the eighteenth century, an array of Deists and Freethinkers, supported by a scholarship which could not be scorned, suddenly appeared on the scene with the contention that if biblical rhetoric were really to be read in a straightforward, honest fashion, it would prove the Bible to be a book like any other book, like Homer or Virgil, and Christianity to be as old as the creation in a sense entirely different from that intended by any Christian.

When eighteenth-century Calvinists had to face such external assaults, they found to their consternation that their internal forces had become unaccountably weakened. Edwards demonstrated his acumen nowhere more strikingly than in the way he went directly to the cause of the weakness. A theory that aims at simplicity should have been capable of a simpler formulation than any Puritan ever quite gave it. If events in nature, being the providence of God, and tropes in the Bible, being the word of God, are specifically intended by Him to convey particular meanings, should they not always make evident one consistent interpretation? If God is speaking through the rising sun or the flowering fruit tree, how can man be secure in understanding if God is saying several things at once? Likewise in the Bible: Solomon may be allegorized or typified as Christ and the Rose of Sharon as the church; but when, for example, I Kings 11:36 says, "That David may always have a lamp before me in Jerusualem," what on earth does it mean? For many crucial passages the Reformation spawned so numerous and such conflicting morals, and some passages yielded up so many successive meanings, and still others so defied all translation, that by 1700 the problem of interpretation was becoming acute. Within provincial New England itself, let alone all Protestantism, the number of disputes, some of them on basic questions, in which opposing sides appealed with equal show of right to the same texts of Scripture, had brought about a crisis in the whole scheme of interpretation that could no longer be ignored. Clearly, something was wrong with the sacred rhetorical theory if it could not be trusted to read the Bible coherently. If the ranks of Protestantism could not be formed anew by a better method of communication with the High Command, they would be scattered before the first charge of the Deistic light cavalry.

To Edwards at this point—and whatever our present religious or stylistic allegiances, I think that on this score we must accompany him—the fatal limitation of the seventeenth-century doctrine became evident. The rhetoric was unprepared to cope with so complex a situation; it had gratuitously assumed certain things which, when called upon to prove, it could not make good. The first Puritans had never really been consistent; while claiming to seek always the one plain teaching of Scripture, they had never expected that all ministers, in preaching upon the same text, would open it in precisely the same way and extract from it, word for word, the same proposition. On the contrary, they actually encouraged a sort of professional rivalry among "learned and judicious persons" concerning favorite texts, on the assumption that different commentators might find different nuggets of significance, all of which could be equally treasured by pious readers. As long as he remained within the "analogy of faith," the Puritan enjoyed a considerable play for impressionism; he was at liberty to report the unique impact that Scripture happened to make on him. If his stimulated imagination found hitherto unappreciated meanings in revelation that would assist others to an "awakening experience," then he had improved his talents. His creative ability had become socially useful as a means of grace. To that extent, subjective freedom was justified.

In New England this amount of rhetorical discretion was sanctioned, was actually encouraged, by the doctrine imported by the founders and still ruling the curriculum at Harvard and Yale during Edwards' time. It came from the French reformer, Petrus Ramus, and had captured the Puritan mind in the English Cambridge before the Great Migration. According to this doctrine, the solid substance of any work, of a poem no less than of a sermon, was its bare logical structure; the rhetoric, which was no more than the tropes and figures, was so much surface ornamentation. It assumed that the mind first framed a proposition about the resurrection, and then bethought itself of the sun as a simile: the simile was not an integral part of the proposition but a separable gem affixed to the logical structure. It could be changed at will. A writer showed his skill by his choice of tropes, but no one theme inevitably demanded a particular simile, and conversely no one image necessarily signified only one proposition. Logic and rhetoric for the seventeenth-century Puritan were distinct categories; the logic was primary, the rhetoric secondary: it was useful but was employable at the discretion of the writer.[6]

For a day when the one concern had been fighting Laud and King Charles, this doctrine was enough; for primitive New England it was enough. It made possible a plain, systematic assertion of doctrine, of which, in New England, Samuel Willard's *The Compleat Body of Divinity,* published in 1726, is the monument. But as the world grew more complex, as the simple theocracy of the seventeenth century became the regionalized, expanding, contentious society of the eighteenth, as winds of new doctrines began to blow and preachers were more and more obliged to entice and cajole their people instead of handing down dogmas, the rhetorical element in the Puritan discourse was more industriously worked. To contrast the prose of Cotton Mather with Bradford's or Hooker's tells the story, perhaps too well, since Mather was the most mannered writer of his generation, though others of the period, Colman and Foxcroft for instance, show almost as clearly how the plain style was becoming more and more figured in an effort to attract a wandering public attention. If the preachers did not take such steps, if they continued in the original style, they ran the risk—most of them in fact succumbed—in the context of the altered society and its augmenting distractions, of preaching in what amounted not to a plain style but a dull.

In response to these pressures there developed in Puritan circles a new rhetorical technique which owed its vogue mainly to the great success of John Flavel's *Husbandry Spiritualized.* This volume, a best seller among nonconformists for a century after its publication in 1669, reversed Bunyan's method: instead of starting with doctrines and clothing them in symbols, it commenced with a segment of actual experience, treated that as the allegory or metaphor, and then, by a burst of ingenuity, extracted an orthodox moral. Each flight took some observed fact of agrarian life and then "spiritualized" it into a doctrine and a homiletic exhortation. Adam had been led by knowledge of God to knowledge of the creature, said Flavel, but now man must learn God by the creature, which meant that he must "spiritualize" the creature, and the more mundane creatures especially. This spiritualizing of common objects, Flavel declared, involves two phases: first an "argumentation," in which an intellectual meaning is read into the objects "by reasoning from them," and second a "meditation," in which an emotional response is elicited by "viewing the resemblance that is betwixt them and spiritual matters."

Thus, the farmer first should "argue" that as he has to wait upon his harvest, so he must wait upon the coming of Christ; and second should "meditate": "This is my Seed-time, Heaven is my Harvest; here I must labour and toyl, and there rest. I see the Husbandmans life is a great toyl; no excellent thing can be obtained without labour, and an obstinate patience," etc.[7] In each act of the spiritualization, the experiential occasion, instead of serving as a metaphor to embellish a thesis, was treated as being itself a metaphor already given, out of which the mind devises significance. It is, for example, a familiar lesson of the farm that industry and diligence are the way to thrive; from this comes an argument: "As nature opens her treasures to none but the diligent, so neither doth grace"; and then a meditation: "Blush then, O my soul, at the consideration of thy laziness and sloath."[8]

The success of the new method was reflected in New England in the 1690's, notably by Cotton Mather, who always responded, as quickly as the means of communication permitted, to London fashions. He and his contemporaries produced a series of tracts which took as their starting points the materials of a trade or handicraft, of the sailor or the carpenter, and resolutely, doggedly spiritualized them. Or else they began with some domestic image, the fire on the hearth or the steam in the kettle. In what frame of mind they labored appears from Cotton Mather's reflecting that, having won success with a booklet spiritualizing the winter, "I thought it would be some service unto Religion to do something at *Summer-Piety*, and make the Objects of the *Summer* subservient unto the Interests of Piety." [9] In 1702 his *Christianus Per Ignem* revealed how highly self-conscious the method had become:

To fetch excellent, and enriching *Instructions* out of the *Creatures* that surround us, is most certainly one of the *Highest Uses* that we can put them unto. . . . And if it *Require* not, yet it will *Produce*, not only *Spirituality* but also *Ingenuity*, more than a little, thus to set all the Creatures of God on speaking unto us. *Truly the Light is sweet*; but usually a *Ray* of *Light* is much the *sweeter*, for descending from Heaven unto us, in some *Earthly Garments* of *Similitude*.[10]

So, giving full reign to his ingenuity, Mather set himself to dress the light of the Gospel in the earthly garment of the household fire, in a work advertised as "never out of season, yet more particularly designed for the seasonable and profitable entertainment of them that would well employ their leisure by the fire-side." One example of Mather's ingenuity will suffice: from the observation that the fire requires air in order to burn, he derived the profitable entertainment that a man who has cares upon his mind should let them have air: "He that has any Remarkable Guilt, lying with distress upon his Conscience, let him single out some *Faithful Pastor*, to whom what he confesses will be as it were but confessed unto the Lord." [11]

That the technique was deliberately cultivated as part of a campaign to reach the masses is shown by a book Cotton Mather published, in avowed emulation of Flavel, in 1727: *Agricola, or the Religious Husbandman.* This appeared with two prefatory recommendations signed by fourteen of the leading ministers of eastern Massachusetts, which were in effect literary manifestoes: "To Spiritualize the Common Actions of Life, and make a religious Improvement of worldly Affairs, is an holy and happy

Art." An application to agriculture was, the ministers agreed, particularly called for "in a Country the Business of which is mostly Husbandry." [12] By this time, ingenuity having become a virtue, Mather's runs riot. The plow is an argumentation of many morals, for instance of "that which brings a *Repenting Sinner* to what we must all come to, that we may find mercy with God. *The Breaking up of the fallow Ground*, with the *Plow*, is, the bringing of the Sinner to that *Repentance* which is necessary for him." [13] Mather was so delighted with his own ingenuity that he sometimes cast the meditation into verse, of a banality which in him amounted to genius:

> Now in Obedience all my Days
> Hard at Work I'll keep,
> Him I'll take pains to please and praise;
> Assur'd, That I shall Reap.[14]

In all the literature of New England there is nothing more tedious than this "spiritualizing." Yet, though it speedily degenerated into a pompous didacticism, it is a profound symptom of the times. Bearing in mind Thomson and Hervey, we may see that this provincial moralizing has, at least in theory, implications that extend beyond Puritanism. The determining influence was undoubtedly the new science, which was demanding respect for fact even from a religious tradition that had once gloried in making fact subserve theology. Puritanism still hungered after allegory, but Cotton Mather was too sophisticated for the simplicity of Bunyan. The result was a compromise that took the form of forcing the symbolical function upon the routine of nature. The power that had once animated the similes of Hooker was evaporating, and a languid generation, no longer capable of creating its images, was becoming enslaved to the images given arbitrarily in experience.

If behind this development can be seen the effects of science, there can also be detected in it an adjustment to the new social environment. Cotton Mather shamelessly gives the game away when he pleads that the art of spiritualizing justifies itself by assisting the life of business: "We may any where, every where, Apply our selves unto it; and especially in the little Fragments of Time that intervene between our more Stated Business." [15] The difference between Mather's "improvements" and Edwards' "shadows" is more than a difference of temperament. Mather and the signers of the prefaces to *Agricola* were men of Boston, where piety had come to terms with mercantile prosperity. To Edwards, their neurotic moralizings were a confession of spiritual poverty. Cotton Mather, we should remember, was held in esteem by Benjamin Franklin because he wrote a book called *Essays to Do Good*. Jonathan Edwards said, "It is one great reason why speculative points are thought to be of so little importance, that modern religion consists so little in respect to the divine Being, and almost wholly in benevolence to men." [16]

In eastern Massachusetts, above all in Boston, men were growing more benevolent, and in the process had so far lost their respect for the divine being that they were openly permitting benevolent writers the liberty of fabricating out of nature whatever meanings would exhibit their ingenuity. The sun itself could be made to serve as a simile not only of the resurrection but of the Reformation, of God's mercy to those who stayed away from taverns, of a successful harvest, or of divine approbation upon the accession of George I to the British throne. A reformation of Puritanism clearly would have to start with a reformation of the Puritan trope.

III. THE CHASTISEMENT OF THE TROPE

WHAT made the task importunate, as the young Edwards appreciated with a clarity of vision unmatched in America, was the fact that in 1687 Sir Isaac Newton had published *Principia*. From the beginning Puritan literature had employed scientific lore as rhetorical embellishment. Out of the similes of the Puritan sermons could be compiled a serviceable handbook on seventeenth-century physics. Inevitably that physics had been Peripatetic, and when the preachers had explained cause and effect, they had expounded Aristotle. But by the end of the century this science was obsolete. A few Puritans had been hesitant about entertaining the "new philosophy" lest it bring with it a "new divinity," but the majority accepted it gradually and complacently. Cotton Mather, as the foremost conservative, guided New England, through his *Christian Philosopher* in 1721, into an adherence to Newtonianism, for he was as adept at spiritualizing phenomena in the new as in the old universe.[17] By the ancient lights of Puritanism, by the canons of the Ramist rhetoric, he was correct. Puritans believed in learning and education. The impulse which produced the Royal Society was nurtured in Puritanism. What had orthodoxy to fear from the substitution of one physics for another? Preachers could illustrate doctrines by analogies in the gravitational field instead of in the predicaments. Surely the metaphorical usefulness of the sun was not altered whether it was held at a given distance from the earth by the revolution of the spheres, or the earth at a given distance from it by a nice adjustment of mathematical forces? Or even in the type: if Joshua was typical of the Church Militant, what difference would a substitution of one scientific version for another make when the preacher drew out the "uses" of the sun's standing still?

For Edwards, it made a difference. That he, more than any of his contemporaries, saw how great a difference, accentuates the lonely grandeur of this isolated figure in the Connecticut Valley, who comprehended in a flash that the old rhetoric would have to be jettisoned if the old physics was dead. There must now be established, he perceived, a closer alliance between the two realms of being, the object in nature or the event in history, and the thesis in the mind. Henceforth the object would enjoy as much claim to authority as the thesis. To Edwards, we may go so far as to suggest, his "Images of Divine Things" was what the *Prelude* was to Wordsworth, a secret and sustained effort to work out a new sense of the divinity of nature and the naturalness of divinity. He was obliged by the logic of his situation to undertake an investigation of the visible world as though no man had seen it before him. When these fugitive notes are read against this background, they take the form of an ambitious project, with the audacious implication suggested in the 26th Image, that if men can properly discover, or rediscover, nature, they may be enabled to employ objects taken from the constitution of the world no longer merely as illustrations of their *meaning*, but as illustrations and evidences of the *truth* of what they say.

To the young Edwards the project seemed feasible because even while he was receiving the vision of mathematical physics he was also granted the revelation of the sensational psychology. At Yale he read John Locke, he later recollected, with a far higher pleasure "than the most greedy miser finds, when gathering up handfuls of silver and gold, from some newly discovered treasure." [18] In the perspective of time the name of Locke has become so associated with the age of prose that we wonder how anyone could ever have become intoxicated with the *Essay Concerning Human Understanding*. But Edwards responded not to the Locke who was to father Utilitarianism but to the Locke who opened for him, as for Berkeley, the vision of a universe organized about the act of perception. That the knowable was confined to the perceptible did not mean for Edwards—whatever it may have meant for Locke—merely that the mind was shut up within five meagre senses; it meant instead a new and exhilarating approach to reality. Once he had grasped that all we know or can know is the idea garnered from the objects of experience, from that point on, whether he spoke of objects as mental or continued (as he saw he might) "in the old way," [19] Edwards was dedicated to the proposition that the relation of mind to object, of truth to embodiment, is intimate, vital, indissoluble. The tangible world, being experienced as ideal, was intelligible only as idea. The facts of experience became for Edwards, as they could not have been even for Hooker or Bunyan, the "shadows," the very "images" of divinity. The act of cognition joined together man and nature, whom scholastic psychology had sundered. As Edwards read the new sensationalism, far from setting up a dualism of subject and object, it fused them in the moment of perception. The thing could then appear as concept and the concept as thing. Although he is customarily represented as an archreactionary Calvinist, Edwards is properly to be described as the first American empiricist; yet from the beginning he, again like Berkeley, recognized that empiricism meant a living relation between man and world, not the dead schematic rationalism from which William James was later to attempt to rescue it. In this way of thinking, the image was no longer a detachable adornment on the surface of truth; it *was* truth. This was the discovery that committed Edwards to a reassertion of Puritan theology in full cognizance of the latest developments in natural philosophy, and to a reassertion of the values of Puritan expression in full awareness of the most recent disclosures of natural psychology. To appreciate what Edwards was attempting in this manuscript, we must read it in full awareness that behind it loom the figures of Newton and Locke. The "Images of Divine Things" was, in the projected "Rational Account," to become a manual of the true style. Equally important with *what* was said would be *how* it was said.

The great virtue of Newtonian science, as Edwards saw it, was that it disciplined the "imagination." He first explained his meaning in the prologue to the "Notes on Science." The prejudices of the imagination, he wrote, are more powerful enemies of truth than any except those of self-interest and impetuous passion, the reason being clear from the Lockean analysis:

For opinions, arising from imagination, take us as soon as we are born, are beat into us by every act of sensation, and so grow up with us from our very births, and by that means grow into us so fast, that it is almost impossible to root them out; being, as it were, so incorporated with our very minds, that whatsoever is objected contrary thereunto, is, as if it were dissonant to the very constitution of them.[20]

What Edwards meant by the imagination was that very "ingenuity" which the old rhetoric had encouraged and the plain style had barely held in check, and then only when the faith had been strong. It was a capriciousness that used God's creation for incidental adornments, that read meanings into things which were no more than what the fancy pretended they might mean. That this ingenuity was still being employed for ornamenting pious morals was no mitigation; the mistake of the fathers was now leading the degenerate children into a welter of spiritualizations which, to the fine sensibility of Jonathan Edwards, were so many vulgarizations.

In the ecstasy of the vision he was to serve until it exhausted him, Edwards resolved within himself that when he would prove anything, he would extricate all questions from confusion and ambiguity "so that the ideas shall be left naked." [21] The naked ideas, not the "flowers of rhetoric"! The error of Cotton Mather and the generation of spiritualizers was that they saw ideas through a haze of imagination. Locke enabled Edwards to define their blunder, and at the same time to see that it could be rectified only by a purification of language: although knowledge does terminate in things, Locke had explained, yet because words interpose themselves so much between the mind and the truth, "like the medium through which visible objects pass, the obscurity and disorder do not seldom cast a mist before our eyes and impose upon our understandings." [22] By opposing naked ideas to the prejudices of the imagination, Edwards in his own way was anticipating the distinction which would be made by post-Kantian philosophers, by Coleridge and Emerson, between the "imagination" and the "fancy," wherein they would promote the imagination to the status of what Edwards meant by the naked idea and leave the fancy substantially what he called imagination. With him as with them, the aim was to establish an activity of mind in which the idea and the object could be so consolidated that the one became expressible in terms of the other.

In Edwards' vocabulary the words "fancy" and "imagination" were still synonymous. In the 174th Image he comments upon the "danger" of being led by the fancy to see images in the "confused appearances" of fire and cloud. After reading Locke, Edwards became an empiricist and ever afterward was to insist, even in his most mystical moments, "there can never be any idea, thought, or act of the mind, unless the mind first received some ideas from Sensation, . . . wherein the mind is wholly passive in receiving them." [23] After studying Newton, Edwards became a mathematical physicist, and always was to insist, as the major premise of all his thinking, "Nothing ever comes to pass without a cause." [24] From these two principles it followed that the physical object, which was the cause of knowledge, could be, of and by itself, apart from being perceived, nothing at all. If the mind is inattentive, whimsical, irresponsible, it will inevitably encounter in nature only "confused appearances." Things have their being by being perceived, and perception is by definition intelligent. Perception sees not dead objects, but by seeing them gives them meaning and direction. Things appear real, he wrote in his "Miscellanies," "because we have a clear idea of them in all their various mutual relations, concurring circumstances, order and dispositions; the consent of the simple ideas among themselves, and with the company of being, and the whole train of ideas in our minds, and with the nature and constitution of our minds themselves." [25] We may doubt whether John Locke would have been altogether happy over his American disciple, but the genius of Edwards consisted in his ability, from the premise of sensationalism, to reach this conclusion: "Seeing the perfect idea of a thing, is, to all intents and purposes, the same as seeing the thing. It is not only equivalent to seeing it, but it is seeing of it; for there is no other seeing but having an idea. Now, by seeing a perfect idea, so far as we see it, we have it." [26] To understand an image, we must see in it reality, not some blurred similitude.

Edwards could so transform Locke's sensationalism, even while remaining a faithful adherent, because he could make the leap which was too strenuous for Locke: if facts do not speak to the passive intelligence merely as what the human mind, in its finitude and its pride, would be pleased to make out of them, then they must come already charged with meaning by an intelligence behind them. Otherwise life would indeed be a play of fancy, a phantasmagoria of men and beasts in insubstantial clouds. Left to itself, the mind will make anything out of everything; but it is not left to itself when it makes out of things exactly what they were intended to mean. Then a circle of intelligibility becomes complete. The absolute significance, variously "shadowed," is rightly caught by the alert, the disciplined, the humble—that is to say, the regenerate—perception. "The way we come by the idea or sensation of beauty is by immediate sensation of the gratefulness of the idea called beautiful." Our grasping it depends not on argument and meditation "but on the frame of our minds whereby they are so made that such an idea, as soon as we have it, is grateful, or appears beautiful." [27] The true man will read nature truly, but false experience will falsify naked ideas. The law for man is not the same as for things, which is both man's glory and his undoing; thing knows thing infallibly by the mechanism of collision, but "nothing is in the mind, or reaches it, or takes any hold of it, any otherwise than as it is perceived or thought of." [28] Simplifying his metaphysics when speaking to his people, Edwards gave them the practical conclusion: "The wonder of unbelievers is such as keeps them from receiving them as true; the mysteries and wonderful things that are displayed in what they hear and see are stumbling blocks to them to prevent their believing." [29]

A knowledge of images, therefore, would be a knowledge not of spiritualized commonplaces but of truth acquired in the only place where, after Locke, it was possible to find it, in sensible experience. To understand the relation of image to truth would be nothing less than to make one's calling and election sure. In literary practice, Edwards' discovery was a Puritan revolt against Puritanism. As against the degraded plain style, with its irresponsible tropes, its reliance on argumentation and meditation, he set up the idea of a pure style. In his art, the rhetorical figures would once more be subjected to the rule of the idea, and the supreme figures would no longer be ingenious compounds of one thing with another but perceptions of the actual identity of those things which are truly united in the eternal system of things.

IV. THE CLARIFICATION OF THE TYPES

WE MAY put it, then, that Edwards in New England was attempting a second reformation. He was attacking the vices of the local
scholasticism just as the reformers had attacked the evils of the
medieval. But in one important maneuver he reversed their
precedent: he turned deliberately to typology. He invoked the
types to rebuke the tropes.

In so doing, he did not need to go back of the reformers to the
medieval typology. He had merely to join himself to a movement already under way. For, in the literature of New England,
during the years in which the moralists were perfecting the art
of spiritualizing the commonplace, a resurgence of typology can
be traced, as it can in the literature of all Protestant com-
munities.[30] It ran parallel to the spiritualizing, and separate, but
was often allied. Probably the increasing demand for sensational
preaching explains both tendencies. To scholars typology may be
a high philosophy, but for the vulgar it has always had a different
though potent attraction, and awareness of its hermeneutical
possibilities becomes a dangerous temptation to preachers who
must stimulate declining zeal. The seventeenth-century revival
was largely inspired by Salomon Glassius' *Philologia Sacra,* published at Jena, 1623–36; for English Puritans the focal work
was *Tropologia: a Key to Open Scripture Metaphors and Types,*
which was a redaction of Glassius brought out in London in 1681
by Benjamin Keach, a nonconformist writer who, even though a
Baptist, was read in New England, where he was favorably
known for his allegorical history of Christianity, *The Travels of
True Godliness.*[31] By the time Edwards began to contend with
the stylistic problem, typology was already being extensively
exploited in the New England sermons, and was being as reck-
lessly indulged as the spiritualizations. If Edwards was to purify
the art of speech in New England, he had not only to chastise
the tropes but to clarify the types.

INTRODUCTION 25

Part of the tragedy of Edwards is that he expended so much
energy upon an effort that has subsequently fallen into contempt.
We are ready to lament that so fertile a mind was beguiled into
wasting itself upon such pedantries as "The things that are said
of the burning bush, do wonderfully agree with the Old Testament representations of the Messiah," or upon making out a case
for Solomon's extension of royal bounty to the Queen of Sheba
being "agreeable to what the prophecies represent of the blessing
and favour of the Messiah to be extended to the Gentiles." [32]
But however preposterous such scholarship may appear to an
age trained in anthropology and historical method, and whatever motives impelled such contemporaries as Benjamin Keach,
Edwards' reasons for turning, with characteristic intensity, to
typology were his own: his newly learned sensationalism, his
newly won conviction of the order of nature, and his perception
that the achievement of a spatial pattern through the Newtonian
physics made imperative the achievement of a corresponding temporal pattern, as Hume and the philosophers of the eighteenth-
century "Heavenly City" were soon to discover. If Edwards was
to find the unity of the Bible, he had also to find the unity of
nature and history in Newtonian and Lockean terms. The one
without the other would be worthless. Newton had found in the
principle of gravity the coherence of nature; a principle for
scriptural interpretation, hitherto as little understood as gravity
had been before Newton, lay ready to hand. So Edwards, who
desperately needed a principle for rescuing religion from the
frivolity of the spiritualizers, since they were succeeding only in
turning it over the faster to Arminians and Deists, seized upon
the types. To understand his action, we may apply to him the
rule which Augustine laid down for understanding typology itself:

In this world of sense, it is indeed necessary to examine carefully what
time and place are, so that what delights in a portion of place or time,
may be understood to be far less beautiful than the whole of which it
is a portion. And furthermore, it is clear to a learned man that what
displeases in a portion, displeases for no other reason than because the

whole, with which that harmonizes wonderfully, is not seen; but that in the intelligible, every part is as beautiful and perfect as the whole.[33]

Edwards' "Images of Divine Things" was to have been part of a whole, and he was responding most creatively to the challenge of his time and place when he set down these observations for a treatise on divine rhetoric. And Pascal had said, a century before him, that from a study of the types there was one clear injunction to be learned: "To speak against too greatly figurative language." [34]

Edwards was only too well aware that an objection could be and had been raised "from the abuse that will be made of this doctrine of types." He knew that it would take the courage of a saint to handle it with impunity. But in so far as a Puritan could be, Edwards was a saint. He wanted to free himself and his people from a worship of idols, he wanted them to perceive. The beauty of a type was exactly that, if it existed at all, it needed only to be seen, not argued. His psychological thesis led him to typology, just as it gave him his program for the correction of New England rhetoric:

The principles of human nature render TYPES a fit method of instruction. It tends to enlighten and illustrate, and to convey instruction with impression, conviction, and pleasure, and to help the memory. These things are confirmed by man's natural delight in the imitative arts, in painting, poetry, fables, metaphorical language, and dramatic performances. This disposition appears early in children.[35]

What at first may seem like a reversion to obscurantism was for Edwards a clarification; having acquired from the empirical psychology an understanding of man's utter dependence on the information of the senses, he was prepared to find in the types not the conjurations they may seem to us but what they had been to Augustine in the first stages of his conversion: "Especially after I had heard one or two places of the Old Testament resolved, and oft times in a figure; which when I understood literally I was slain spiritually." [36]

Had Edwards, even with Locke to assist him, done no more than create a new typology, he might deserve mention in a history of American scholarship, but he would amount to no more than a footnote in any account of the American mind. His originality is not that he led a typological revival in America; his readings of the types within the Bible seem to be quite traditional. What gives his undertaking a wider interest was his effort to extend the method into nature and history. Coming to it as both a Lockean and a Newtonian, he appropriated for analogical treatment whole portions of nature which hitherto, in New England at least, had been utilized only for similitude and metaphor. The regenerate man was one who could perceive; what he saw, in the clarity of purified vision, was idea; an idea in the Bible was a signification of divine intention expressed through a type. Therefore did it not follow that the seeing man could behold the intentions of God expressed in the universe through the types of nature? In nature, said Edwards, the agreement between the animal creation and the divine idea would be exactly the same *kind* of agreement as between the types of the Old Testament and their antitype. "There is an harmony between the methods of God's providence in [the] natural and religious world." [37] Here was the central perception about which Edwards strove to organize God's creation: the Bible is only one among several manifestations of the typical system; the pattern of the cosmos is infinite representation, and thereby intelligible.

The system of created being may be divided into two parts, the typical world, and the antitypical world. The inferiour and carnal, i.e. the more external and transitory part of the universe, that part of it which is inchoative, imperfect, and subservient, is typical of the superiour, more spiritual, perfect, and durable part of it which is the end, and as it were, the substance and consummation of the other. Thus the material and natural world is typical of the moral, spiritual, and intelligent world, or the city of God. [38]

That Edwards concluded this remarkable passage with the Augustinian phrase does not necessarily indicate that he was familiar with Augustine, of whom I can find little direct influence in his writings; but in what tradition Edwards, by the sheer force of genius, was working becomes clear when we compare his words with Augustine's: "O Wisdom, Thou most sweet light of the cleansed mind; for Thou ceasest not to intimate to us what and how great Thou art, and these intimations of Thee is the universal beauty of creation." [39] To show the coherence of a universal beauty, Edwards began compiling his list of intimations, which he could alternatively think of as "the language and lessons of nature, or as the true city of God."

This extension of typology, reinterpreted by the new science and psychology, was the starting point for a restatement of theology. It was an innovation in New England Puritanism, in Protestantism, because he proposed to mold the mind into the closest possible relation with natural objects, as a glove upon a hand. But in that very proposal was implied a still more radical break with the past: an exaltation of nature to a level of authority coequal with revelation—nature as seen by the regenerate eye, but still nature, the nature of the *Principia*. His would be no mere mechanical substitution of one physics for another, eliciting no more than unctuous moralizing. Cotton Mather, like his father and grandfather, was unaware of either the scientific or moral hazards he ran in using natural images to decorate a doctrine. He had not grasped the immensity of the intellectual revolution; he was still living, despite his reading of Newton, in the mental world of Calvin, who had taught the Puritans that when believers hear the syllables of the Bible it is as though "they heard the very words pronounced by God Himself," but that from the realm of nature, though it is a mirror in which they are given clear representations of God, they can get no real advantage because of their stupidity.[40] "For as soon as a survey of the world has just shown us a deity, neglecting the true God, we set up in his stead the dreams and phantasms of our own brains." [41] But Edwards learned from Newton that henceforth nature could be slighted only at the peril of our life. Man, for all his stupidity, had managed to read the three laws of motion as well as the ten commandments. The spiritualizations of nature were phantasms, but the *Principia* were not. Nature—or history, which is nature in time—was not a disjointed series of phenomena; it was a living system of concepts, it was a complete, intelligible whole. Edwards' theology was not dogma, it was an indirect confession that for him, as for all men after him, nature had become as compelling a way of God's speaking, if God speaks at all, as Scripture. The passion with which he strove to heed this voice is reflected in the compression of these fragments. They testify how Edwards, who in certain moods was exhilarated at the prospect, in others was terrified. Unless nature and Scripture could be, in some sense, integrated, man would be left with a set of religious axioms that would no longer bear any meaningful relation to the rules he now knew were governing the universe.

As I read these notes, viewing them as a part of his uncompleted "Account," they say that Edwards, by seeking so relentlessly for the shadows of divine things in occurrences, was highly resolved not to let science itself, as a mere description of phenomena, take the place of a philosophy or theology of nature. Neither was he ready to turn his back on the flux, to seek reality in a supersensuous realm of essences separate from things. The Lockean empiricism bound him to the earth. He undertook, therefore, with a courage that must be admired whatever we may think of the result, to solve his problem by finding in things an intelligibility not transcending them but immanent in them. Whatever generalizations he would believe in and worship—the naked ideas—would be conceived in reference not to some merely imaginable order but always to the order of objects. The proper reading of science (with all its phenomenal content) and of history (with all its fluctuations) would be metaphysical. Yet he had also learned enough of scientific method and empirical psychology to be certain in advance that no theology of nature could give rules to science. The thesis he labored to vindicate in these notes was that empirical science—the "type"—embodies over and over again the ontological truth—the "antitype." Fully, joyfully accepting the new science, Edwards was resolved that it should not be permitted to exist apart from philosophy, not so much because he was committed to certain intellectual vested interests as because he perceived that a science which was not a science of intelligibles was no science at all. It would be of no use whatever to mankind, who are intelligent and must live with intelligibles. So he set himself to expound the universe in such a manner that nature and history might be viewed as infinite repetitions of a few eternal rules, which, however, were to be learned only in the objects. Spiritual truths would thus not be illustrated by objects, but objects would be an endless, experimental restatement of the truths.

In other words, for Edwards the real problem was not theological but scientific, and this investigation of images was a series of experiments. The question was, how far into nature and history might he legitimately push the typological method? He had no intention of abolishing rhetoric. It would still be permissible to compare, on a purely subjective basis, one thing with another, as Edwards did in his sermons with great skill, most notably, not to say notoriously, at Enfield, when he compared humanity to a spider loathed by the God who suspends it over the fiery pit. Edwards was not so foolish as to attempt to correct an abuse of metaphors by a denial of all metaphor. But it was necessary, considering the triumphs of mathematical science, to draw the line with nice precision between what could be used in metaphor and what might be seen as a type. The issue was so fundamental that he frequently felt obliged to face it in his pulpit, from which, in keeping with his youthful resolve "to be very moderate in the use of terms of art," [42] he generally excluded the concerns of his study. When, for instance, he preached upon the metaphors under which the Bible represents the punishment of the wicked—the blackness of darkness, the worm that never dies, the fire—he was obliged to explain that by the loose standards then prevailing in New England these expressions might be discounted as merely "rhetorical." "If they should be taken in an equality to the literal sense, it would carry the matter beyond the strict truth." To this objection Pascal had said, "When the word of God, which is really true, is false literally, it is true spiritually." Edwards' way of saying it was to point out that when scriptural metaphors are applied to temporal things, as they sometimes are, they are hyperbolical: "Where the Scripture uses metaphors and similitudes about temporal things, it only does it for the beauty of expression." So in human speech, metaphors derived, as all metaphors must be, from the appearances of nature, are legitimate, and then the only rule that governs them is "beauty of expression." But when we speak of "spiritual things," we are no longer using images merely according to the rules of stylistic felicity. When so employed, language has entered into a different realm, where conventional rhetoric no longer holds; in this realm figurative statements must be austerely handled only as types.[43] Otherwise the imagination, the chief instrument of Satan, perverts the very act of perception.

Thus, to say that virtue shines like the sun is permissible, for then we are speaking rhetorically, in the consciousness that our simile is composed of elements acquired through the senses. But to carry the light of the sun into the realm of spirit as a similitude is to invite disaster. Light in the language of "shadows" is not a metaphor, it is an "image."

Thus persons are deceived by the use of figurative and metaphorical expressions. When we speak of light let into the soul in this case, nothing is meant of any resemblance to any brightness that we see with our bodily eyes, of the nature of brightness of the sun or any other shining object; this is a very gross notion of spiritual light, such light is not spiritual but outward. Spiritual light is the light of the mind. The light of the mind is knowledge, truth and evidence. It is a sight, sense, and a right understanding of things that is spiritual light. When a person is made to understand spiritual things in a new manner, and is convinced of the truth of them, and has a realizing apprehension of them, and lively sense of their excellency, then he has new light. That conviction of the judgment, and that sense of heart are called light only figuratively, not that there is any proper visible shining or anything that looks like the shining of some distant object. Not but that persons when under the lively sense of the glory of spiritual objects may naturally continue in their minds a lively idea of an outward glory and brightness.

But that is only an idea in the imagination, and is not the thing that the essence of spiritual light consists in.[44]

At the end of Edwards' quest, the distinction he sought between the trope and the type was this: the trope may be a lively notion of an outward thing, and so be useful in social intercourse, in business or in preaching, but the shadow or the image must be that of which the spiritual reality consists in itself. And the two must never, under pain of damnation, be confused.[45]

Among the "Miscellanies," where so much of Edwards' best thought is still entombed, there is a further hint of what the types meant for him. He is asking himself how one mind can know another. By whatever means heavenly intelligences may communicate, in this world one mind can know another mind only mediately, by some sign or manifestation. The ways of mediate communication are four. We, being intelligences ourselves, may argue the contents of another's mind a priori, on the analogy with ourselves. We may rationally and inductively conclude from certain effects or actions of the other what is going on in his mind. We may listen to his words and take what he says, according to our credence of his veracity, as what he means. Or, we may gauge him by his "images or resemblances." Images are not similarities, actions, or words; they are the signs of one intelligence interpreted by another: "its air and motions, of the sense and affections of the mind . . . something that is intended on purpose for a representation of him." For Edwards, this way of knowing, this form of divination, is the ultimate way. And by these ways we may come to know not only the minds of men but the mind of God. We may argue a priori from the necessity of His existence and perfections—for Edwards this "ontological" argument is the least rewarding and plays little part in his thinking. We may draw conclusions about Him as cause from our experience of His effects—the conventional "theism from design" argument, which Edwards handles, when discussing it apart from the images, in a conventional eighteenth-century fashion. We may listen to His spoken word—this is to take the Bible as plain speech, which is necessary with the multitude because the types and shadows "are hard to be understood." But we may also "see Him in images." That there exists this last approach, different from ontology, design, and revelation, is Edwards' peculiar and inspired conception. His emphasis, as always, is upon the verb. To see is to apprehend. Any dullard with the help of a little logic can argue a priori; any scholar can repeat the argument from design, and all men can read or hear read the Bible. But to *see* the visible symbols of His presence in "anything that being from him has some resemblance of him, as the sun's majesty and green fields and pleasant flowers of his grace and mercy," and also in "the soul of man that is made in the image of God"—this *seeing* is the supreme act of humanity.[46] In a post-Newtonian, post-Lockean world, it is the highest possible form of communication. The grace of God is what enables the vision: it is, to borrow the language of Wordsworth, with whom Edwards offers so many startling parallels, "a master light of all our seeing."

It should be noted, to avoid a confusion against which Edwards does not always defend the reader, that when he distinguishes between an effect and an image, he often intends a difference in the perceiving of an object rather than a difference of objects themselves. The sun, when serving as the principal exhibit in the argument from design, is not the same sun that is seen as an image. Images are, so to speak, the overtones of effects registered in the human consciousness. Edwards has a habit of shifting, suddenly and without warning, an effect into type. Yet the distinction in his mind is always clear: it is a difference of seeing. In 1736 he explained to his people in Northampton, "A merely rational opinion, that there is a God from the consideration of the works of creation, is cold, and does not reach the heart." But the view of the saints which gives an image along with an effect, or which can make an effect appear as an image, is a different sort of perception:

And sometimes, when the soul is full of the spirit of God, wherever they turn their eyes, if they look up to heaven, or if they look on the face of the earth, still there seems to be a cast of the glory of God to be seen in things. Sometimes this effect arises from beholding some particular part of the creation. Sometimes it may be in beholding the sun, or in viewing the moon walking in her brightness, or in seeing the stars in their height and glory, or in looking at the clouds and sky, or in viewing the face of the earth, with the works of God upon it, the trees, grass, and flowers. Sometimes it may be such a particular thing as the singing of birds, or seeing other creatures which God has made for us.[47]

The world of these things, sun, moon, stars, and singing birds, is still for Edwards, as it was for Augustine and Calvin, mutable and corruptible. Yet their real being is not in mutability or corruption; it is in the metaphysical realities of which they are the shadows Edwards' contention is that the metaphysical realities, though capable of abstract statement, exist only in the infinite shadows of the physical world, where intelligence, if it is pure, may read them as naked ideas. Nature thus interpreted becomes a principle of activity; the perceiving mind, taken in a completely empirical sense as wholly "passive," participates in matter as a voluntary intention. Human intelligence, the image of the intelligence that informs nature, finds in mutability not a mass of confused appearances but analogical traces of the deep realities, the intentions of God. Human perception of these analogies is the human response to divine conversation. A man who sets himself to reason without divine light is like a man who, going into a garden at night, compares things together by feeling his way from plant to plant and measuring the distances: "But he who sees by divine light is like a man that views the garden when the sun shines upon it. There is, as it were, a light cast upon the ideas of spiritual things in the mind of the believer which makes them appear clear and real which before were but faint obscure representations." [48]

The book that Edwards dreamed of making out of these notations might have been the crown of his system. If the images were God speaking compellingly, as Newton now obliged all men to admit they might be, if it were possible to speak of them with a rigorous suppression of ingenuity, if the mind could be disciplined so as not to lump them together to suit fashionable modes, then a book of images and shadows would set forth the spiritual universe, just as the *Principia* had set forth the material. A catalogue of the language and lessons of nature would be more than a handbook of rhetoric; if done objectively, humbly, it would be a dictionary of the divine discourse.

The sublime and the pathetic fact about Jonathan Edwards is that he believed he could do it. The arrogance and the humility of the man are both in this manuscript. We are in the secret of his being when we comprehend how on the one hand he humbled himself, as few Christians succeed in doing, to a realization that only God can speak for Himself, but on the other hand enjoyed the magnificent assurance that he, solitary in pioneer America, could accurately report the vocabulary of the deity's monologue. The passion, the pride, the power, and the weakness of Puritanism are compacted in the works of Edwards as in no other American writer. It took a major artist to go so unerringly to the heart of his problem, and this incomplete sketch of what would have been as great a work as any he published helps to make clear why Edwards was indeed the pre-eminent spokesman for his tradition. What wider validity the notes may have must depend on the suffrage of a wider audience, if such exists, than one interested merely in Puritanism. The central contention has, it seems to me, a value quite apart from its connection with the historical background. The manuscript asserts, even in its present form, that whatever can be said of the inexpressible glory will be said, can in fact only be said, in the dialect of created things. It may be, Edwards wrote in one of his finest meditations, that when we come to heaven we shall know forms of beauty inconceivable to us now; but while we linger on this earth,

We can conceive of nothing more beautiful of an external kind than the beauties of nature here, especially the beauty of the more animated parts of this world. We never could have conceived of these if we had not seen them; and now, we can think of nothing beyond them; and therefore the highest beauties of art consist in imitation of them.[49]

V. FORESHADOWINGS

WHATEVER may be the worth of this manuscript today, there can be no doubt that in relation to time and place, if the force of these factors is acknowledged as Augustine has urged upon us, it is instructive as pertaining not only to the previous history of New England but also to what followed, in New England, in America, in Protestantism. Edwards was dramatically shifting the traditional emphasis: he was quoting Scripture to confirm the meaning of natural phenomena, not adducing natural images to confirm the meaning of Scripture. He would indignantly have denied that he was setting nature above revelation, and most of his life's work was expended in proving the folly of those who did. Nevertheless, the fresh vision with which he had started was this: "Our Senses, when sound, and in ordinary circumstances, are not properly fallible in any thing. . . . When our Senses make such or such representations, we constantly experience that things are in themselves thus or thus." [50] The innovation in such thinking was actually a revolution in sensibility; it was nothing less than an assertion of the absolute validity of the sensuous. In the lifelong elaboration of the "Miscellanies" the implications of this apprehension were irresistibly drawn out. He concluded his section on the nature of images, from which we have already quoted, with a reflection more explicit than any he permitted himself to publish:

The manifestations God makes of Himself in His works are the principle manifestations of His perfections, and the declaration and teachings of His word are to lead to these. By God's declaring and teaching that He is infinitely powerful and wise, the creature believes that He is powerful and wise as He teaches, but in seeing His mighty and wise works, the effects of His power and wisdom, the creature not only hears and believes, but sees His power, and wisdom, and so of His other perfections. [51]

Therefore, unless men could be brought to perceive the power and wisdom of God in nature, to which the power and wisdom of the revealed word was, as Edwards secretly confessed, subordinate, Christian culture was threatened with a fatal division of authority. In the face of such a prospect, Edwards strove to perfect a universal language for nature, history, and Scripture, an idiom that would be common to all and that could also be comprehended by such intelligences as ours, which must learn the little they can learn from the sensible, by that wonderful alchemy of perception in which the soul makes metaphysical meanings out of mechanical vibrations that reach the eye or ear. The conception of images as a form of communication, distinct from words, inductions, and syllogisms, seemed to him an answer. It may be that his concrete answer is now of no more than archeological interest, but it must be acknowledged that Edwards did define if he did not solve the problem.

Yet even he never recognized how much his age was being swept along in a current of sensibility to destinations he dreaded. The deification of nature which Newton made not so much possible as imperative removed the last restraints which historical Christianity had imposed upon an identification of the moral and the natural. If all the interplay of things is actually a more commanding form of God's speaking than edicts handed down on Mt. Sinai—even if it is only just as commanding—then the traditional warnings against making an idol out of nature are pushed aside. If nature is not simply a vast effect from which skilled dialecticians argue a cause, but is an image in which men may perceive what for them is divine, sooner or later the veneration of nature will become secularized; the way will be opened for an uninhibited enjoyment of it—and also for an unrestrained exploitation. Within three generations of Edwards a child of the Puritan tradition, who was to say that if he was the devil's child he would live from the devil (even though he managed to live as a saint), was to find warrant for an unqualified naturalism in the certainty that the "ethical character so penetrates the bone and marrow of nature, as to seem the end for which it was made." [52] Emerson signalized the destruction of the balance of the factors which Edwards strove to maintain, and there seems little prospect of its being restored in New England or in America.

That Edwards would have scorned the Emersonian naturalism goes without saying. That he would have understood Hawthorne immediately seems to me equally obvious. Yet when we look upon Edwards, considering the trend of the modern centuries, he must appear a phase in a development which was not confined to pulpits. It is no diminution of his genius, it is rather a recognition, to say that he was, on the deepest level of his being, moving with the times. That he poured his consciousness into the ungrateful molds of theology was an accident of history; what gave vitality to his thinking was not the logic of his polemical tracts but the intensity of his love for a universe that divinity had made and in which divinity was immanent. If experience had demonstrated that the doctrine of the plain style concealed an ambivalence toward ingenuity, and if he was able to recognize how that ambivalence had betrayed it, yet in his own attitude toward nature Edwards was condemned to a still greater equivocation. As a doctrinaire Calvinist he was obliged to see in the material world a gigantic *memento mori*, yet he loved that world, and his passion for it dominated even his most abstract reasoning. His love was no less intense because, even to himself, he could express it only obliquely. The indirect perception of beauty, to which he had to make resort (frank celebration of the senses being denied him), took the form of a direct perception of types.

We may therefore be emboldened to draw out as the ultimate signification of this text a moral which would have embarrassed the author. The orginal Puritan doctrine of expression, admirable though its results often were, was after all not sufficiently Puritanical. While it permitted the Puritan artist a certain liberty to concoct metaphors and similes at will, at the same time it inhibited the exercise of private judgment, which in fact, though not always in profession, was the heart of Puritanism. The rhetorical theory assumed that the Bible had already done man's thinking for him; all he had to do was to employ his ingenuity in finding illustrations or making applications. It was, in short, an instrument of authoritarianism and of dogmatism. When

Edwards went back to typology, he was invoking a method which, with all its extravagances, had for generations been a cryptic, often an unconscious, protest against authority. Modern rationalists may dismiss typology as an absurdity, but during the long ages when theology was the jealous queen of the sciences, typology had served as a rallying point for rationality, and the debt which the modern mind owes to it is immense even though unacknowledged. On the surface typology appeared to abandon the intellect to the tyranny of the Bible even more than did the ordinary forms of exegesis; yet by a stratagem that was not always unintentional it introduced into the very citadel of theology, into the word of Jehovah, the criterion of a coherent dialectic. The typologist, even in his worst vagaries, was seeking a pattern of repetition, the recurrence of eternal verities, not the caprices of fiat; he strove to wrest from Scripture, even when the prospect was least encouraging, a system based upon the enduring traits of mind and not upon brute dogma. Though seemingly devoted to the letter of Scripture, by reading design and progress into the biblical narrative, typology paradoxically furnished a protest against literalism. The reformers' distrust of it was, considering their premises, altogether justified; so poetic a rendering of the Bible as Edwards was here seeking would mean the end of bibliolatry. Mad though it often became, typology somehow had kept alive at least a semblance of humanism, and now in the eighteenth century Edwards, probably not altogether aware of how really vast was the tradition behind it, turned to it in order that he might find the supernatural scheme of redemption articulated in terms compatible with the natural order.

It was to this suspect and dangerous science that Edwards, the arch-Calvinist of America, resorted in his most secret moments. He revered the will of God, and he schooled himself into delighting to ascribe absolute sovereignty to the Creator. But he was also, though far removed from European capitals, a man of the eighteenth century, and he was aware, at least as much aware as Franklin, of what a revolution the human reason had wrought within Christendom by the end of the seventeenth century. But still more important is the fact that Edwards was also an original, a creative spirit, a man of passion, of vision, of Miltonic grandeur. After studying his manuscript, the reader may indeed wonder whether Edwards recognized that in reverting to typology he was actually furthering the revolution, that while professing to be a Calvinist he was reaching out for a method of interpreting both revelation and providence in which the governing principle would be not the will of God but the insight of Jonathan Edwards. Possibly had he seen such implications in this undertaking, he would have suppressed it. Perhaps because, to some extent, he did sense them, he kept the manuscript private and enigmatic. But whatever the degree of his awareness, when he wrote down these images, his mind was working without the help of formulae or of orthodox platitudes. It was an exercise in private judgment with a vengeance. He was striving, against immense handicaps, to express a new vision of the world in which the conflict of the spirit and the flesh, of the divine and the rational, which has shattered and still shatters European culture, could be resolved into a single perception of beauty. For that reason it has seemed advisable to print along with the "Images or Shadows of Divine Things" an extract from another unpublished fragment which concludes with the astounding confession that the Puritan priest who so unpityingly consigned the visible world to an ultimate conflagration on the Day of Judgment thoroughly comprehended that men hate to die because they cannot bear to let go the beauty of this world.

VI. THE EARTHLY IMAGE

On the simpler level of biographical and sociological reference, the manuscript has considerable interest. Reflections of Edwards' experience in the Great Awakening of 1740, his immense hope that it might be something approaching the millennium, his theory of the "outpouring" of the eternal spirit in time, and his bitter disillusion with the results, are clearly evident in the sequence of the notes. In the last sections he often copies out pas-

sages from other writers; the later entries in the voluminous
"Miscellanies" are likewise made up of extracts, which suggests
that his own inspiration was tiring. In both manuscripts he often
copies portions of authors who were opposed to his doctrines,
and it may be that he insisted to himself, despite the evidence,
that in these paragraphs they really meant what he meant. But
everywhere the writer of these notes is the same person who in
his boyhood exhibited a power for the meticulous observation
of "The Spider." The pure passion of his love for common
things appears at every point, as do many other facets of his
temperament that invite a less admiring analysis. Whether his
abhorrence of water as a symbol along with his appreciation of the
river is entirely a consequence of his typology or of some obscure
twist in his own psychology had best be left to those more capable than I of diagnosing such symptoms. No one can fail to perceive the realism, not to say the brutality, which is always a
strength of Puritan writers; his description of spring in the
152d Image may offend sensibilities trained in romantic literature, but it is a more accurate image of that season in New England than all the poetry of Whittier and Longfellow. The
style, even allowing for the state of the manuscript, is wholly
characteristic of Edwards, especially the repetitions, which seem
in part to be a carry-over from his pulpit manner, but are also
an evidence of his fascination with language as a species of in-
cantation. And finally, though Edwards was the last man in the
world to be trusted with reporting the social or economic elements
in his civilization, yet because he sought for images in the most
familiar facts about him, many of these reflections testify to the
quality of life in the agrarian, hard-working, excitable Connecticut Valley of the mid-eighteenth century.

IMAGES OR SHADOWS
OF
DIVINE THINGS

1. Death temporal is a shadow of eternal death. The agonies, the pains, the groans and gasps of death, the pale, horrid, ghastly appearance of the corps, its being laid in the dark and silent grave, there putrifying and rotting and become exceeding loathsome and being eaten with worms (Isa. 66.24), is an image of the misery of hell. And the body's continuing in the grave, and never rising more in this world, is to shadow forth the eternity of the misery of hell.

2. (Vid. Image 46.) We are all clothed with the fleeces of sheep. We are clothed with the righteousness of the Lamb (Acts 8.32), as a lamb dumb before his shearers. We were all Christ's crucifixion, our sins crucified him; as we are his shearers, we by his sufferings, which our sins brought on him, get his fleece to clothe ourselves withall.

3. Roses grow upon briars, which is to signify that all temporal sweets are mixt with bitter. But what seems more especially to be meant by it is that pure happiness, the crown of glory, is to be come at in no other way than by bearing Christ's cross, by a life of mortification, self-denial, and labour, and bearing all things for Christ. The rose, that is chief of all flowers, is the last thing that comes out. The briary, prickly bush grows before that; the end and crown of all is the beautifull and fragrant rose.

4. The heavens' being filled with glorious, luminous bodies is to signify the glory and happiness of the heavenly inhabitants,

and amongst these the sun signifies Christ and the moon the church.

5. Marriage signifies the spiritual union and communion of Christ and the church, and especially the glorification of the church in the perfection of this union and communion forever. (Vid. Images 9, 12, 56.)

6. The blood comes from the heart, to intimate that out of the heart are the issues of life. (Prov. 4.23.)

7. That the things of the world are ordered [and] designed to shadow forth spiritual things appears by the Apostle's arguing spiritual things from them, I Cor. 15.36: Thou fool, that which thou sowest is not quickened except it die. If the sowing of seed and its springing were not designedly ordered to have an agreeableness to the resurrection, there could be no sort of argument in that which the Apostle alledges, either to argue the resurrection itself or the manner of it, either its certainty or probability or possibility. See how the Apostle's argument is thus founded (Heb. 9.16, 17) upon the validity of a testament.

8. Again it is apparent and allowed that there is a great and remarkeable analogy in God's works. There is a wonderfull resemblance in the effects which God produces, and consentaneity in His manner of working in one thing and another throughout all nature. It is very observable in the visible world; therefore it is allowed that God does purposely make and order one thing to be in agreeableness and harmony with another. And if so, why should not we suppose that He makes the inferiour in imitation of the superiour, the material of the spiritual, on purpose to have a resemblance and shadow of them? We see that even in the material world, God makes one part of it strangely to agree with another, and why is it not reasonable to suppose He makes the whole as a shadow of the spiritual world? (Vid. Image 59.)

9. Again as to marriage, we are expressly taught that there is a designed type of the union between Christ and the church. (Eph. 5.30, 31, 32. Vid. Images 5, 12, 56.)

10. Children's coming into the world naked and filthy and in their blood, and crying and impotent, is to signify the spiritual nakedness and pollution of nature and wretchedness of condition with which they are born.

11. The serpent's charming of birds and other animals into their mouths, and the spider's taking and sucking the blood of the fly in his snare are lively representations of the Devil's catching our souls by his temptations.

12. We are told that marriage is a great mystery, as representing the relation between Christ and the church. (Eph. 5.32.) By mystery can be meant nothing but a type of what is spiritual. And if God designed this for a type of what is spiritual, why not many other things in the constitution and ordinary state of human society and the world of mankind? (Images 5, 9, 56.)

13. Thus I believe the grass and other vegetables growing and flourishing, looking green and pleasant as it were, ripening, blossoming, and bearing fruit from the influences of the heavens, the rain and wind and light and heat of the sun, to be on purpose to represent the dependence of our spiritual wellfare upon God's gracious influences and the effusions of His holy spirit. I am sure there are none of the types of the Old Testament are more lively images of spiritual things. And we find spiritual things very often compared to them in Scripture.

14. The sun's so perpetually, for so many ages, sending forth his rays in such vast profusion, without any diminution of his light and heat, is a bright image of the all-sufficiency and everlastingness of God's bounty and goodness.

15. And so likewise are rivers, which are ever flowing, that empty vast quantities of water every day and yet there is never the less to come. The spirit communicated and shed abroad, that is to say, the goodness of God, is in Scripture compared to a river, and the trees that grow and flourish by the river's side through the benefit of the water represent the saints who live upon Christ and flourish through the influences of his spirit. (Jer. 17.8; Ps. 1.3; Num. 24.6.)

16. I don't know but that there are some effects commonly seen in the natural world that can't be solved by any of the general laws of nature, but seem to come to pass by a particular law for this very end to represent some spiritual thing, particularly that of serpents' charming of birds and squirrels into their mouths. (Vid. Image 43.)

17. In its being so contrived that the life of man should be continually maintained by breath, respect was had to the continual influence of the spirit of God, that maintains the life of the soul. (Image 62.)

18. Women travail and suffer great pains in bringing children forth, which is to represent the great preparations and sufferings of the Church in bringing forth Christ and in increasing the number of his children, and a type of those spiritual pains that are in the soul when bringing forth Christ.

19. (Vid. Misc. 362.¹) So it is God's way in the natural world to make inferiour things in conformity and analogy to the superiour, so as to be the images of them. Thus the beasts are made like men; in all kinds of them there is an evident respect had to the body of men, in the formation and contrivance of their bodies, though the superiour are more in conformity and the inferiour less. Thus they have the same senses, the same sensitive organs, the same members, head, teeth, tongues, nostrils, heart, lungs, bowels, feet, etc. And from the lowest animal

to the highest, you will find an analogy, though the nearer you come to the highest, the more you may observe of analogy. And so plants, that are yet an inferiour sort of beings, they are in many things made in imitation of animals: they are propagated by seed which produce others of the same kind; the earth answers to the womb; there is something that answers to generation in the flower; there is a male part that impregnates the female part. The time of blossoming is as it were the time of love and pleasure, being the time of generation, when the seed and fruit are, as it were, conceived. They are like animals in their growing by nourishment, running in veins, in suffering and dying by wounds, and [in] some of them there is an image of sensitiveness.

20. See how the Apostle argues, I Cor. 15. from the 36th to the 42d verse.

21. The purity, beauty, sublimity, and glory of the visible heavens as one views it in a calm and temperate air, when one is made more sensible of the height of them and of the beauty of their colour, when there are here and [there] interposed little clouds, livelily denotes the exaltedness and purity of the blessedness of the heavenly inhabitants. How different is the idea from that which we have in the consideration of the dark and dire caverns and abyss down in the depths of the earth! This teaches us the vast difference between the state of the departed saints and of damned souls; it shows the ineffable glory of the happiness of the one and the unspeakeable dolefullness and terrours of the state of the other. (See Image 212.)

22. The wise-man argues from an image in the natural world, Eccles. 1.7: All the rivers run into the sea, yet the sea is not full. (See it by me explained.)

"Notes on the Scriptures," [2] Eccles. 1.7, No. 461: It appears by the connection of these words with what went before that the design of the wise-man is here to signify that the world, though it be so full of labour, mankind from generation to generation so constantly, labouriously and unweariedly pursuing after happiness and satisfaction or some perfect good wherein they may rest, yet they never obtain it, nor make any progress towards it. Particular persons, while they live, though they spend their whole lives in pursuit, do but go round and round, and never obtain that satisfying good they seek after. The eye is not satisfied with seeing nor the ear with hearing (verse 8), and as one generation passes away and another comes (verse 4), the successive generations constantly labouring and pursuing after some good wherein satisfaction and rest may be obtained, not being discouraged by the disappointments of the former generations, yet they make no progress; they attain to nothing new beyond their forefathers. They only go round in the same circle, as the sun restlessly repeats the same course that it used to do in former ages, and as the wind and water, after their running and flowing, have got no further than they were formerly, for to the place from whence they came they constantly return again, and as the sea is no fuller now than it used to be in former ages, though the rivers have all that while, with constant and indefatigable labour and continual expence of their waters, been striving to fill it up. That which goes round in a circle, let it continue moving never so swiftly and never so long, makes no progress, comes to nothing new.

23. (Vid. John 12.24.) Verily, verily, I say unto you, except a corn of wheat fall into the ground and die, it abideth alone, but if it die, it bringeth forth much fruit.

24. The head is after a peculiar manner the seat of the soul, though the soul be also in the whole body. So the Godhead dwells in the man Christ Jesus bodily. He dwells also in believers by way of participation with the head. (Vid. Misc. 487.[3])

25. There are many things in the constitution of the world that are not properly shadows and images of divine things that yet are significations of them, as children's being born crying is a signification of their being born to sorrow. A man's coming into the world after the same manner as the beasts is a signification

of the ignorance and brutishness of man, and his agreement in many things with the beasts.

26. Christ often makes use of representations of spiritual things in the constitution of the [world] for argument, as thus: the tree is known by its fruit. These things are not merely mentioned as illustrations of his meaning, but as illustrations and evidences of the truth of what he says.

27. The waves and billows of the sea in a storm, and the dire cataracts that come of rivers, have a representation of the terrible wrath of God and amazing misery of [them] that endure it. Misery is often compared to waters in the Scripture, a being overwhelmed in waters. God's wrath is compared to waves and billows, Ps. 88.7; 42.7; Job 27.20: Terrors take hold as waters; Hos. 5.10: I will pour out my wrath upon them like water. In Ps. 42.7, God's wrath is expressly compared to cataracts of water: Deep calleth unto deep at the noise of thy water-spouts. And the same is represented in hail, stormy winds, black clouds, and thunder, etc.

28. As thunder and thunder clouds, as they are vulgarly called, have a shadow of the majesty of God, so the blue skie, the green fields, and trees, and pleasant flowers have a shadow of the mild attributes of God, viz., grace and love of God, as well as the beauteous rainbow.

29. When we travail up an hill, it is against our natural tendency and inclination, which perpetually is to descend. And therefore, we but go on ascending with labour and difficulty. But there arises a pleasant prospect to pay us for our labour as we ascend; and as we continue our labour in ascending, still the pleasantness of the prospect grows. Just so is a man paid for his labour and self-denial in the Christian course. (Vid. Image 67.)

30. If God had so much regard to the names of persons, that they might signify things chiefly remarkeable concerning them,

why should we think He would not in His ordering the nature of things have respect to spiritual things, so as to signify and represent them?

31. I do believe that it is so ordered that such an extraordinary degree of heat should be necessary in order to refine metals that it might represent the exceeding fierceness of God's wrath and the extremity of the sufferings by which the dross of the world is consumed, and the saints (who are the gold) are saved as the metal delivered from its oar and dross by the heat of the furnace. So the saints are saved from their sins by the suffering in their head, Jesus Christ, the dire wrath of God.

32. It is ordered so that there should be in man's nature a foundation laid for so strong and dear a love towards a woman, if a suitable object and occasion present, to represent the exceeding love of Christ to his church; and that man's jealousy of unchastity in the woman beloved should be so violent and cruel a passion to represent the jealousy of Christ towards his people when he sees them give that to other lovers which belongs to him alone.

33. The extreme fierceness and extraordinary power of the heat of lightning is an intimation of the exceeding power and terribleness of the wrath of God.

34. Young twigs are easily bent and made to grow another way, old trees most difficultly. So persons in youth are more easily turned than others. Again, a young plant is much more easily plucked up by the roots than after it hath long stood and is rooted deep in the ground. So it is more easy to forsake sin in the beginning than after a long continuance in it.

35. The silk-worm is a remarkeable type of Christ, which when it dies yields us that of which we make such glorious clothing. Christ became a worm for our sakes, and by his death kindled

that righteousness with which believers are clothed, and thereby procured that we should be clothed with robes of glory. (Vid. Image 46. See II Sam. 5.23, 24; and Ps. 84.6: The valley of mulberry trees.)

36. See notes on Eccles. 1.5, etc.

"Notes on the Scriptures," Eccles. 1.5: The sun also ariseth: Those kinds of vicissitudes in earthly things show the imperfections of earthly good in these respects:

1. It is good that is sought by this labour of the creature, by the labour of the sun and wind and streams, they are labouring for good. But by their restlessness therein, still continuing to labour, it appears that they don't fully attain their end, they don't attain any sufficient good. If they did, they would leave off labouring as having attained what they labour for: as what the rivers aim at by their running is to fill up the sea, but by their still continuing to run, they go back to the same place and run the same course again, it appears they do not do it.

2. By their doing the same work over and over, it appears that they not only don't attain any sufficient good, but they don't make progress towards it. There is nothing new. . . . The rivers not only don't fill up the sea, but they don't gain upon it. . . .

3. It shows the unsatisfying nature of earthly good thus that when one kind has been enjoyed a little while, there is need of change. After the light of the sun has been enjoyed a little while, then something else is sought, night, and perhaps it is desired. After summer has been enjoyed a while and the wind blowing from the south, then winter is desired and the wind from the north. We can't live upon one sort of earthly enjoyment but we must have change continually.

4. And as it shows the unsatisfying nature of earthly good, so it shows its exceeding fleeting, fading nature. It is an evidence of the great imperfection in it that after it has been enjoyed a little while it don't only perish in the enjoyment but turns to ill, to that which is lothsome, so that the contrary is desired. After the light of the sun has been enjoyed a little, it is troublesome and darkness is desired. After we have been awake a little while, it is burdensome, we want to sleep, and then we are weary of that and want to be awake again. When a man [eats] that which gratifies his appetite, it presently grows irksome, he desires no more of it for the present.

37. See notes on Job 41.34

"Notes on the Scriptures," Job 41.34: He is a king over all the children of pride: i.e., mystically: he whom the Leviathan was under to be a type of, viz., Satan is king over all the children of pride.

38. See notes on Genesis 15.5.

"Notes on the Scriptures," Gen. 15.5: The stars were designed by the creator to be a type of the saints, the spiritual seed of Abraham, and the seeming multitude of them, which is much greater than the real multitude of visible stars, was designed as a type of the multitude of the saints.

39. See Misc. No. 635, concerning searching and launcing a wound in order to a cure.

"Miscellanies," No. 635: Bad wounds must be searched to the bottom; and oftentimes, when they are very deep, they must be launced, and the core laid open, though it be very painful to endure, before they can have a good cure. The surgeon may skin them over, so that it may look like a cure without this, without much hurting the patient, but it will not do the patient much good. He does but deceive him for the present; but it will be no lasting benefit to him, the sore will break out again. This figures forth to us the case of our spiritual wound, the plague of our hearts which is great and deep and must be searched, must be launced by painful conviction; the core must be laid open; we must be made to see that fountain of sin and corruption there is, and what a dreadful state we are in by nature, in order to a thorough and saving cure; Jer. 8.11, speaking of the teachers of Israel, their prophets and priests: They have healed the hurt of the daughter of my people slightly, saying, Peace, Peace, when there is no peace.

40. The gradual vanishing of shades when the sun approaches is a type [of] the gradual vanishing of Jewish ordinance as the Gospel dispensation was introduced. (Vid. Misc. No. 638.)

"Miscellanies," No. 638: There is an harmony between the methods of God's providence in [the] natural and religious world, in this as well as many other things: that, as when day succeeds the night, and the one comes on, and the other gradually ceases, those lesser lights that served to give light in the absence of the sun gradually vanish as the sun approaches; one star vanishes after another as daylight increases, the lesser stars first and the greater ones afterwards, and the same star gradually vanishes till at length it wholly disappears, and all these lesser lights are extinguished and the sun appears in his full glory above the horizon. So when the day of the Gospel dawned, the ceremonies of the Old Testament and ordinances of the law of Moses, that were only appointed to give light in the absence of the sun of righteousness, or until Christ should appear, and shone only with a borrowed and reflected light, like the planets, were gradually abolished one after another, and the same ordinance gradually ceased, and those ordinances that were principal (one of which was the Jewish sabbath) continued longest. There were a multitude of those ceremonies, which was a sign of their imperfection; but all together did but imperfectly supply the place of the sun of righteousness. But when the sun of righteousness is come, there is no need of them; when the true sacrifice is come, there is no need of any of the legal sacrifices; when Christ is come, and gives and introduces the Gospel, that is, the ministration of the Spirit, there is no more need of ceremonies in worship, but the time is now come that men must worship God in spirit and in truth. So there is a multitude of stars that shine in the night; but they altogether do but very imperfectly supply the absence of the sun; but when the sun rises they all vanish, and we find no want of them.

41. Children's coming to their inheritance by the death of their parents and by their will and testament, which becomes of force by their death, is a designed type and shadow of believers' receiving their inheritance by the free and sovereign disposal and gift of God in His Word, which is His testament or declaration of His will with respect to the disposal of His goods or the blessings He has in store for men. And believers come to the possession thereof by the spirit of Christ. This is evident by the Apostle's arguing from it, Heb. 9.15–17.

42. The gradual progress we make from childhood to manhood is a type of the gradual progress of the saints in grace, and the gradual progress the church makes towards perfection of knowl-

edge, holiness, and blessedness, as seems by the Apostle's arguing in the I Cor. 13.11: For when I was a child I spake as a
child, I understood as a child; but when I became a man, I put
away childish things.

43. (Vid. Image 16.) It is a great argument with me that God,
in the creation and disposal of the world and the state and course
of things in it, had great respect to a shewing forth and resembling spiritual things, because God in some instances seems to
have gone quite beside the ordinary laws of nature in order to
it, particularly that in serpents' charming birds and squirrels
and such animals. The material world, and all things pertaining
to it, is by the creatour wholly subordinated to the spiritual and
moral world. To show this, God, in some things in providence,
has set aside the ordinary course of things in the material world
to subserve to the purposes of the moral and spiritual, as in
miracles. And to show that all things in heaven and earth, the
whole universe, is wholly subservient, the greater parts of it as
well as the smaller, God has once or twice interrupted the course
of the greater wheels of the machine, as when the sun stood still
in Joshua's time. So, to shew how much He regards things in
the spiritual world, there are some things in the ordinary course
of things that fall out in a manner quite diverse and aliene
from the ordinary laws of nature in other things, to hold forth
and represent spiritual things.

44. Vid. notes on Isa. 28.24, etc.

"Notes on the Scriptures," Isa. 28.24: What is designed here seems to
be that God deals with His people as a prudent husbandman with his
field and with his grain, for God's people are His husbandry, I Cor. 3.9.
Christ says his Father is the husbandman, John 15, and under this
comparison God shows what is the reason of the afflictions and judg-
ments that He brings upon them. God in the preceding part of the
chapter had been setting forth the judgment that should be brought
on the land; He here teaches the gracious design He had in it to His
people, as it is common through this prophecy to intermix threatnings

of judgment with promises of succeeding mercy. Herein God deals with His people as a prudent husbandman deals with his field: at first he plows his field and breaks the hard clods, and makes smooth the roughness of it, makes plain the face of it, and so frees and removes it, and then sows his seed. So God by the afflictions He brings on His people, He doth as it were plow and mellow the hard ground, and breaks the hard clods and evens their roughness to fit them to receive the seed and to bring forth good fruit. And as the plowman plowes the ground no more and no longer than is needfull to fit it for the seed, . . . so God will afflict His people no more and hold them under affliction no longer than to fit them for spiritual good.

And as the husbandman suits his seed to his ground, he casts on the wheat in the principal place, . . . and the barley and rice into the ground that is suitable for them, so God deals with His people. He deals with every one according to their kinds, deals forth those blessings that are most fit for them; that which is fit for one is not fit for another. Every one has his distinct sort of gifts and brings forth their different sort of fruit, each one according to his capacity, temper or circumstances. If the husbandman has this discretion in managing his field, much more shall He have in dealing with His people who gives the husbandman that discretion and is the bestower of all wisdom and prudence.

Truly God deals with His people in the afflictions He brings upon them as the husbandman deals with his grain when he threshes it. The end of his threshing, it is not to break or bruise the grain, but to cleanse it, to separate it from the husk and fit it for the owner's use: so God's end in the afflictions He brings on His people is not to injure His people, but to purify them and to separate them from their sins and wean them from the world and fit them for God's use. And as the husbandman uses discretion in threshing his grain, one sort of grain he threshes in one manner and another in another, as shall best suit the several sorts of grain and tend most to separating of it from the husk without bruising it; and the husbandman shows his descretion also in the degree of his threshing, he won't be ever threshing it, he will thresh no longer than until he has separated the grain, and not so as to bruise it: so God deals wisely with His people in the degree and kind of afflictions He brings on them. He will bring various afflictions on various sorts of persons that are suitable for them, and He will afflict them no more than is for their good. Thus is God wonderful in counsel and excellent in working, and does every thing in the wisest and best manner. God's people are elsewhere called His grain and His harvest, and the like.[4]

45. That natural things were ordered for types of spiritual things seems evident by these texts: John 1.9, This was the true light, which lighteth every man, that cometh into the world; and John 15.1, I am the true vine. Things are thus said to be true in Scripture in contradistinction to what is typical: the type is only the representation or shadow of the thing, but the antitype is the very substance and is the true thing. Thus, heaven is said to be the true holy of holies, in opposition to the holy of holies in the tabernacle and temple, Heb. 9.24: For Christ is not entered into the holy places made with hands, which are figures of the true, but into heaven itself, now to appear in the presence of God for us. So the spiritual Gospel tabernacle is said to be the true tabernacle, in opposition to the legal, typical tabernacle, which was literally a tabernacle, Heb. 8.2: A minister of the sanctuary and of the true tabernacle, which the Lord pitched and not man, and that though the legal tabernacle was much more properly a tabernacle according to the literal meaning of the word than the other. So Christ is said to be the true bread from heaven, in opposition to the manna that was typical, though that was literally bread from heaven, John 6.32: Then Jesus said unto them, Verily, verily, I say unto you, Moses gave you not that bread from heaven, but my Father giveth you the true bread from heaven. So, in those fore-mentioned text[s], it is evidently in the same sense that Christ is said to be the true vine and the true light of the world, and is the true vine, in opposition to vines literally so called, which are types, the union and dependence of whose branches on the stock and root is a type of the union and dependence of Christ's members on him. So he is the true light of the world in opposition to the sun, the literal light of the world that is a type of the sun of righteousness. (See Dan. 7.16.)

46. We in our fallen state need garments to hide our nakedness (having lost our primitive glory), which were needless in our

state of innocency. And whatsoever God has provided for mankind to cloath themselves with seems to represent Jesus Christ and his righteousness, whether it be anything made of skin or the coats of skins that God made our first parents represented the righteousness of Christ, or the fleeces of sheep, it represented the righteousness of him who is the Lamb of God and who was dumb as a sheep before his shearers. And the beautifull cloathing from the silk-worm that the worm yields up at his death represents the glorious clothing we have for our souls by the death of him who became a man, who is a worm and the son of man, who is a worm and who said he was a worm and no man. And the flax with which we are clothed seems well to represent the spiritual clothing we have by Christ: that small, weak, feeble, and mildewed [plant] but well represents him who grew up as a tender plant, as a root out [of] a dry ground, wherein was no sin or guiltiness; it is exceedingly bruised and broken and beaten with many blows, and so yields us its coat to be our cloathing. And Christ, through exceeding great suffering, yields us his righteousness, that is as fine linnen, clean and white, and presents us without a spot to the Father. (Vid. Images 2 and 35.)

47. That the earth is so small a thing in comparison of the distance between it and the highest heaven that, if we were there, not only the high palms and highest mountains would look low, whose height we gaze and wonder at now, but the whole earth would be less than nothing, nothing could be seen of it. Yea, if it were many million times bigger than it is, yea, probably many millions of millions times, it would probably be too small a speck to be seen, i.e., it would still be less than nothing. It seems to typifie how that worldly things, all worldly honour and pleasure and profit, yea, the whole world and all worldly things put together, is so much lower and less than heavenly glory. Then when the saints come to be in heaven, all will appear as it were infinitely less than nothing.

48. Corn must be first ground to powder before it is fit for our food. So Christ must first suffer very extremely, even to death,

and a very dreadfull death, before we can receive spiritual nourishment by him. The execution of God's wrath is compared to this very thing by Christ, viz., grinding to powder by a stone (Matt. 21.44). Hence meal is used as a type of Christ (II Kings 4.41); Elisha cast meal into the poisoned pottage and healed it. So corn must be baked in the oven or by the heat of the fire before it is fit for our nourishment, and all our food almost is prepared by fire, which has respect to Christ, our spiritual food, his being prepared to be our food by suffering the fire of God's wrath. (Vid. Image 68.)

49. The trial of gold and silver in the fire is a type of the trying of saints and their graces by persecution and other occasions of suffering and self-denial for God's sake, whereby the gold and silver is not only found to be pure, but is refined and purified more from dross and made much better. So those trials of the saints not only prove their sincerity, but refines them, purges away their dross, strengthens their graces, and purges them from impure mixtures.

50. The rising and setting of the sun is a type of the death and resurrection of Christ. (Vid. notes on Deut. 21.23 and Luke 23.44.)

"Notes on the Scriptures," Deut. 21.23: His body shall not remain all night upon the tree, but thou shalt surely bury him the same day: The manner of the Israelites in pursuance of this institution used to be to let them hang until the sun was down and then to take the bodies down and bury them. . . . It is very probable that one reason why those that were hanged and accursed were to be taken down and buried as soon as the sun was down was that the sun was a type of Christ, and in setting was a type of the death of Christ. . . . The corpse was to be removed and buried as soon as the sun was set, to signify that the curse is removed by the death of Christ, for he in dying was made a curse for us and the curse by his death is taken from the earth, or at least from the land of Israel or the land of the church, so that that land is not defiled.

"Notes on the Scriptures," Luke 23.44: He who made the sun to be a type of Christ saw meet that when Christ died that should be darkened, that while Christ's sufferings on the cross continued and he was deprived of joy and comfort the sun should be deprived of light. That the sun is a type of Christ was probably one reason why Christ's resurrection was about the time of the rising of the sun, i.e., because the rising of the sun is a type of the resurrection of Christ, as the sun setting is a type of the death of Christ; . . . and the rising of the sun happens so often, it is no sign that it is not a type of the resurrection of Christ that is but once, for it is fit that the type should be repeated often but that the antitype should be but once.

51. As the death of the body is a type of the second death, spiritual and eternal death, so the stinking of a dead corpse is a type of that first in Prov. [10.7]: The name of the wicked shall rot. It is a type of that everlasting shame and contempt and abhorrence that the damned shall be the subjects of signified by that [in] Isa. 66.24: And they shall go forth and look upon the carcasses of the men that have transgressed against me, for their worm shall not die; neither shall their fire be quenched, and they shall be an abhorring to all flesh. (Images 1, 61.)

52. The flame of a candle or lamp, the manner of its burning when first lighted up with a feeble light, the ways of extinguishing of it, its being so easily put out by a breath or blast of wind, its being drowned by its own oil that feeds it when there is an excess of it, the manner of lighting one by another, the manner of its going out when burnt out, seems designed by providence to represent the life of man, I Kings 11 ⅀6: That David may always have a lamp (or candle) before me in Jerusalem; I Kings 15.4: Nevertheless for David's sake did the Lord his God give him a lamp *or candle* in Jerusalem; so II Kings 8.19; II Chron. 21.7; Job 18.6: His candle (or lamp) shall be put out with him; Job 21.17: How oft is the candle (or lamp) of the wicked put out, and how oft cometh their destruction upon them? So Prov. 13.9: 24.20; and 20.20.

53. The different glory of the sun, moon, and stars represents the different glory of Christ and the glorified saints. The sun repre-

sents Christ, the moon well represents the glory of the prophets and apostles and other ministers of Christ that have been improved as such lights of his church and instruments of promoting and establishing his kingdom and glory, and so have been luminous to enlighten the world by reflecting the light of the sun that is of Christ, and conveying his beams to them. And possibly the blessed virgin, who in another respect was the instrument of bringing this light to the world, but yet in such a respect that the other [meaning] is conveyed, for they are called Christ's mother: they travail in birth till Christ is formed and brought forth, they are the great instrument of bringing forth the man-child in the sense in which it is spoken in Rev. 12.5. (See notes on Cant. 2.11, the second part of the note; see note on I Cor. 15.42.[5])

54. As the sun, by rising out of darkness and from under the earth, raises the whole world with him, raises mankind out of their beds, and by his light, as it were, renews all things and fetches them up out of darkness, so Christ, rising from the grave and from a state of death, he, as the first begotten from the dead, raises all his church with him, Christ the first fruits and afterwards they that are Christ's at his coming. And as all the world is enlightened and brought out of darkness by the rising of the sun, so by Christ's rising we are begotten again to a lively hope, and all our happiness and life and light and glory and the restitution of all things is from Christ rising from the dead, and is by his resurrection.

55. That the works of nature are intended and contrived of God to signify and indigitate spiritual things is particularly evident concerning the rainbow, by God's express revelation.

56. (Vid. Images 5, 9, 12.) Eph. 5.30, 31, 32: For we are members of his body, of his flesh, and of his bones. For this cause shall a man leave his father and mother and shall be joined unto his wife, and they two shall be one flesh. This is a great mystery, but I speak concerning Christ and the church. By this passage of

Scripture it is evident that God hath ordered the state and constitution of the world of mankind as He has to that end that spiritual things might be represented by them. For here the Apostle tells us that it is so ordered of God that a man should leave his father and his mother and cleave to his wife for this cause, viz., because Christ is so closely united to the church (for it is much the most natural so to understand it). And then, in the next words says, This is a great mystery, but I speak concerning Christ and the church, a great mystery, i.e., a mysterious typical representation which refers ultimately to the union between Christ and the church. God had respect to Adam and Eve as a type of Christ and the church when He took Eve out of Adam and gave that institution mentioned in Genesis.

57. It is very fit and becoming of God, who is infinitely wise, so to order things that there should be a voice of His in His works, instructing those that behold them and painting forth and shewing divine mysteries and things more immediately appertaining to Himself and His spiritual kingdom. The works of God are but a kind of voice or language of God to instruct intelligent beings in things pertaining to Himself. And why should we not think that He would teach and instruct by His works in this way as well as in others, viz., by representing divine things by His works and so painting them forth, especially since we know that God hath so much delighted in this way of instruction.

58. (Join this to Misc. Nos. 362 and 370.) It is a sign that the beautifull variety of the colours of light was designed as a type of the various beauties and graces of the spirit of God that divine and spiritual beauties and excellencies are so often represented in Scripture by beautifull colours. Thus particularly the colours of the rainbow are made use of, as has been shewn [in] Miscell[anies] Nos. 362 and 370. So it was in the colours of the precious stones of the breastplate of the High-Priest, in which were red, yellow, green, blue, and purple, and by the colours of the precious stones of the foundations and gates of the New Jerusalem, in which were

all those same colours. (See Thomson's *Cyclopaedia*.) The foundations, gates, windows, and borders of the church of the City of God are said to be of such precious stones in Isa. 54.11, 12, and God there promises to lay her foundations in fair or beautifull colours. So the temple of Solomon was beautified with precious stones of various beautifull colours (I Chron. 29.2). God's appearance is said to be as of a jasper and sardius stone (Rev. 4.3); a jasper is green sometimes and sometimes purple, sometimes of many colours (See Chambers [6]), and a sardius which is red. So the light of the New Jerusalem is said to be as of a stone most precious, even a jasper stone (Rev. 21.11); the streets of the city were as pure gold like unto clear glass. So the hangings of the tabernacle and temple, and the ephod and breastplate were of blue, purple [and] scarlet. Thus the amiable beauties and graces of the spirit of God are represented by various beautifull colours to the eye in the same manner, as by the various sweet spices of the holy anointing oil and the sweet incense, and the various sweet odours of the different spices and sweet fruits so often spoken of in Solomon's Song. So Joseph's coat of many colours represents the various spiritual beauties and graces of his robe of righteousness. (See Sermon on Acts 7.9, etc.[7])

The various colours of the light of the sun signifies the various beauties of the spirit of God in two respects and are so made use of in Scripture: 1. To represent the moral goodness of God (which, as it is in God, is the same with the Holy Ghost), as variously expressed and manifested in several attributes, as justice, truth, goodness, mercy, patience, and the like; 2. To represent the virtues and graces in the saints that are the various exercises and fruits of the spirit in their hearts.

White, which comprehends all other colours, is made use of in Scripture often to signify holiness, which comprehends all moral goodness and virtue, sometimes to denote the holiness of God, as Rev. 19.11; Matt. 17.2; Rev. 20.11, and elsewhere, and sometimes the holiness or righteousness of the saints, either imputed or inherent, Rev. 3.4, 5, and 18; 4.4; 7.9, 13; 15.6; 19.8, 14.

There is a variety in light. One and the same white light,

though it seems to be an exceeding simple thing, yet contains a very great variety of kinds of rays, all of so many different excellent and lovely appearance. So the same simple spirit of God seems to contain a great variety, and therefore He is in Revelation called seven spirits. There is one body, one spirit, and yet a vast variety of gifts, I Cor. 12.4: Now there are diversities of gifts, but the same spirit, and verse 11: All these worketh that one and self-same spirit.

"Miscellanies," No. 362: There is yet more of an image of the Trinity in the soul of man: there is mind, and its understanding or idea, and the will or affection or love: answering to God, the idea of God, and the love of God.

Indeed, the whole outward creation, which is but the shadows of His being, is so made as to represent spiritual things. It might be demonstrated by the wonderful agreement in thousands of things, much of the same kind as between the types of the Old Testament and their antitypes; and by there being spiritual things being so often and continually compared with them in the word of God. And it is agreeable to God's wisdom that it should be so, that the inferior and shadowy parts of His works should be made to represent those things that are more real and excellent, spiritual and divine, to represent the things that immediately concern Himself and the highest parts of His work. Spiritual things are the crown and glory, the head and soul, the very end, the alpha and omega of all other works. So what therefore can be more agreeable to wisdom than that they should be so made as to shadow them forth. And we know that this is according to God's method, which His wisdom has chosen in other matters. Thus the inferior dispensation of the Gospel was all to shadow forth the highest and most excellent which was its end; thus almost everything that was said or done, that we have recorded in Scripture from Adam to Christ, was typical of Gospel things. Persons were typical persons; their actions were typical actions; the cities were typical cities; the nations of the Jews and other nations were typical nations; their land was a typical land; God's providences towards them were typical providences; their worship was typical worship; their houses were typical houses; their magistrates, typical magistrates; their clothes, typical clothes, and indeed the world was a typical world. And this is God's manner to make inferior things shadows of the superior and most excellent; outward things shadows of spiritual;

and all other things shadows of those things that are the end of all things, and the crown of all things. Thus God glorifies Himself and instructs the minds that He has made.

"Miscellanies," No. 370: We have a lively image of the Trinity in the sun: the Father is as the substance of the sun; the Son is as the brightness and glory of the disk of the sun, or that bright and glorious form under which it appears to our eyes; the Holy Ghost is as the heat and powerful influence, which acts upon the sun itself, and being diffusive, enlightens, warms, enlivens and comforts the world. The Spirit, as he is God's infinite love and happiness, is as the internal heat of the sun; but, as he is that by which God communicates Himself, he is as the emitted beams of God's glory: II Cor. 3.18: But we all with open face, beholding as in a glass, the glory of the Lord, we are changed into the same image, from glory to glory, even as by the Spirit of the Lord. That is, we are changed to glory, or to a shining brightness, as Moses was, from or by God's glory or shining, even as by the Spirit of God, i.e., which glory or shining is the Spirit of the Lord. The word that is translated FROM with respect to glory, and BY with respect to the Spirit, is the same in the original, it is both, and therefore would have been more intelligibly translated: We are changed BY glory into glory, even as BY the Spirit of the Lord. Moses was changed by God's glory shining upon him, even as we are changed by God's Spirit shed as bright beams on us.

The Spirit of God is called the Spirit of glory, I Peter 4.14: If ye be reproached for the name of Christ, happy are ye; for the Spirit of glory and of God resteth upon you: on their part he is evil spoken of, but on your part he is glorified. The Spirit of glory resteth upon you, upon two accounts, because it is the glory of God, and as it were His emitted beams, and as it is the believer's glory, and causes him also to shine.

The various sorts of rays of the sun and their beautiful colours do well represent the Spirit, and the amiable excellency of God, and the various beautiful graces and virtues of the Spirit. The same we find in Scripture are made use of by God for that purpose, even to signify and represent the graces and virtues of the Spirit. Therefore I suppose the rainbow was chosen to be a sign of the covenant. And St. John saw a rainbow round about those of God, . . . and a rainbow upon the head of Christ. . . . And I believe the variety that there is in the rays of the sun, and their various beautiful colours were designed in the creation for this very purpose.

59. (Add this to Image 8.) If there be such an admirable analogy observed by the creatour in His works through the whole system of the natural world, so that one thing seems to be made in imitation of another, and especially the less perfect to be made in imitation of the more perfect, so that the less perfect is as it were a figure or image of the more perfect, so beasts are made in imitation of men, plants are [a] kind of types of animals, minerals are in many things in imitation of plants. Why is it not rational to suppose that the corporeal and visible world should be designedly made and constituted in analogy to the more spiritual, noble, and real world? It is certainly agreeable to what is apparently the method of God's working.

60. That of so vast and innumerable a multitude of blossoms that appear on a tree, so few come to ripe fruit, and that so few of so vast a multitude of seeds as are yearly produced, so few come to be a plant, and that there is so great a waste of the seed of both plants and animals, but one in a great multitude ever bringing forth anything, seem to be lively types how few are saved out of the mass of mankind, and particularly how few are sincere, of professing Christians, that never wither away but endure to the end, and how of the many that are called few are chosen.

61. Ravens, that with delight feed on carrion, seem to be remarkeable types of devils, who with delight prey upon the souls of the dead. A dead, filthy, rotten carcass is a lively image of the soul of a wicked man, that is spiritually and exceeding filthy and abominable. Their spiritual corruption is of a far more loathsome savour than the stench of a putrefying carcass. Such souls the Devil delights in; they are his proper food. Again, dead corpses are types of the departed souls of the dead and are so used. (Isa. 66.24.) Ravens don't prey on the bodies of animals till they are dead; so the Devil has not the souls of wicked men delivered into his tormenting hands and devouring jaws till they are dead. Again, the body in such circumstances being dead and in loathsome putrefaction is a lively image of a soul in the dismal state it is in under

eternal death. (See Image 151.) Ravens are birds of the air that are expressly used by Christ as types of the Devil in the parable of the sower and the seed. The Devil is the prince of the power of the air, as he is called; devils are spirits of the air. The raven by its blackness represents the prince of darkness. Sin and sorrow and death are all in Scripture represented by darkness or the colour black, but the Devil is the father of sin, a most foul and wicked spirit, and the prince of death and misery.

62. (Vid. Image 17.) The natural life is continually supported by the breath that enters into the vitals, by which is represented how the spiritual life is constantly maintained by the spirit of God entering into the soul. And therefore one is used as a type of the other in the Scripture, as particularly in Ezek. 37.9, 10: Prophesy unto the wind, prophesy, son of man, and say unto the wind, Thus saith the Lord God: Come from the four winds, O breath, and breath[e] upon these slain, that they may live. So I prophesied as he commanded me, and the breath came into them, and they lived, and stood up upon their feet an exceeding great army. Together with verses 13, 14: And ye shall know that I am the Lord, when I shall have opened your graves, O my people, and brought you up out of your graves, and shall have put my spirit in you, and you shall live; John 20.22: He breathed on them and saith unto them, Receive ye the Holy Ghost.

63. In the manner in which birds and squirrels that are charmed by serpents go into their mouths and are destroyed by them, is a lively representation of the manner in which sinners under the Gospel are very often charmed and destroyed by the Devil. The animal that is charmed by the serpent seems to be in great exercise and fear, screams and makes ado, but yet don't flee away. It comes nearer to the serpent, and then seems to have its distress increased, and goes a little back again, but then comes still nearer than ever, and then appears as if greatly affrighted, and runs or flies back again a little way, but yet don't flee quite away, and soon comes a little nearer and a little nearer with seeming fear and distress that

drives them a little back between whiles, until at length they come so [near] that the serpent can lay hold of them and so they become their prey. Just thus often times sinners under the Gospel are bewitched by their lusts. They have considerable fears of destruction and remorse of conscience that makes them hang back, and they have a great deal of exercise between while, and some partial reformations, but yet they don't flee away. They will not wholly forsake their beloved lusts but return to them again. And so, whatever warnings they have and whatever checks of conscience that may exercise them and make them go back a little and stand off for a while, yet they will keep their beloved sin in sight and won't utterly break off from it and forsake [it], but will return to it again and again and go a little further and a little further, until Satan remedilessly makes a prey of them. But if any one comes and kills the serpent, the animal immediately escapes. So the way in which our souls are delivered from the snare of the Devil is by Christ's coming and bruising the serpent's head.

64. Hills and mountains are types of heaven, and often made use of as such in Scripture. These are difficultly ascended. To ascend them, one must go against the natural tendency of the flesh; this must be contradicted in all the ascent, in every step of it, and the ascent is attended with labour, sweat and hardship. There are commonly many hideous rocks in the way. It is a great deal easier descending into valleys. This is a representation of the difficulty, labour, and self-denial of the way to heaven, and how agreeable it is, to the inclination of the flesh, to descend into hell. At the bottom of valleys, especially deep valleys, there is water, with a lake or other waters, but water, as has been shown elsewhere in notes on Scripture, commonly signifies misery, especially that which is occasioned by the wrath of God. So in hell is a lake or gulf of misery and wrath.

65. Eccles. 3.21: Who knoweth the spirit of man that goeth upward, and the spirit of a beast that goeth downward to the earth? The wise man there seems to have evident respect to the manner

of the breath's going forth in death in men and beasts by the posture they are commonly in when dying, as a type that the spirit or soul of man returns to God that gave it (Chap. 12.7), and the spirit of a beast to the earth where the body goes, that it ceases to be, comes to nothing, as the body does that putrifies and turns to earth.

66. (Vid. Image 64.) Hills and mountains, as they represent heaven, so they represent eminence in general, or any excellence and high attainment. And as hills, especially high mountains, are not ascended without difficulty and labour, and many rocks and steep places are in the way, so men don't attain to any thing eminent or of peculiar excellence without difficulty.

67. (Vid. Image 29.) He that is travelling up a very high mountain, if he goes on climbing, will at length get to that height and eminence as at last not only to have his prospect vastly large, but he will get above the clouds and winds, and where he will enjoy a perpetual serenity and calm. This may encourage Christians constantly and steadfastly to climb the Christian hill. The perfect and uninterrupted serenity and calm there is on some very high mountains is also a type of the heavenly state. (See Image 158.)

68. (Vid. Image 48.) As wheat is prepared to be our food, to refresh and nourish and strengthen us, by being threshed and then ground to powder and then baked in the oven, whereby it becomes a type of our spiritual food, even Christ the bread which comes down from heaven, which becomes our food by his sufferings, so the juice of the grape is a type of the blood of Christ as it is prepared to be our refreshing drink, to exhilarate our spirits and make us glad, by being pressed out in a winepress. The pressure of a winepress is that to which the suffering of the wrath of God is often compared in Scripture. And because our bread made of wheat and our wine made of the juice of the grape are thus types of Jesus Christ as given for our meat and drink by his sufferings and the sacrifice of himself, therefore this bread and wine

in Deut. 32.14, is called the fat of the kidneys of wheat and the pure blood of the grape, in an evident allusion to those parts of slain beasts that were offered to God in sacrifice, that were by God's law appropriated to Him and wholly offered to Him, as being the most essential parts of the sacrifice. For the fat of the kidneys and the blood of their sacrifices were things which by divine appointment were parts of their sacrifices so appropriated. So oil, that great type of the grace of the Holy Spirit, is procured by treading and pressing the olives. (Mic. 6.15.) But the Holy Spirit is the sum of all the benefits of Christ procured for us by his sufferings.

Coroll[ary]: Hence we learn how fitly bread and wine were chosen to represent the body and blood of Christ in the Lord's Supper. (See further concerning that text, Deut. 32.14: Images 149, 189.)

69. Some of the most poisonous kinds of serpents have their tongues for their weapon, wherewith they naturally sting others, and serpents commonly therefore with their tongues do represent the venomous nature of the tongues of wicked men, and how much the corruption of the heart flows out by that member, and in how venomous and deadly a manner it is put forth thereby. And therefore it is said of wicked men that the poison of asps is under their tongues, and the Apostle James says the tongue is full of deadly poison, Jas. 3.6, and that it is a fire, a world of iniquity, and setteth on fire the course of nature and is set on fire of hell, etc. And the Ps. 140.3: They have sharpened their tongue like a serpent.

70. If we look on these shadows of divine things as the voice of God purposely by them teaching us these and those spiritual and divine things, to show of what excellent advantage it will be, how agreeably and clearly it will tend to convey instruction to our minds, and to impress things on the mind and to affect the mind, by that we may, as it were, have God speaking to us. Wherever we are, and whatever we are about, we may see divine things excellently represented and held forth. And it will abundantly tend

to confirm the Scriptures, for there is an excellent agreement between these things and the holy Scripture.

71. It is from littleness of soul that the mind is easily disturbed and put out of frame by the reproaches and the treatment of men, as we see that little streams of water are much disturbed in their course by small unevennesses and obstacles that they meet with, and make a great deal of noise as they pass over them, whereas great and mighty streams would pass over them calmly and quietly with smooth and unruffled [surface]. Prov. 16.32: He that is slow to anger is better than the mighty and he that rules his spirit than he that takes a city.

72. When God began to make the world and put it into order and cause light to shine, it was a chaos, in a state of utter confusion, without form, and void, and darkness was upon the face thereof. So commonly things are in a state of great confusion before God works some great and glorious work in the church and in the world, or in some particular part of the church or world, and so oftentimes towards particular persons. Any very great and remarkeable work of God is in Scripture commonly compared to a work of creation. And before God appears in such a work and so causes light to shine, things are commonly in a most dark, confused and wofull state, and appear most remote from anything that is good, and as if there was no hope of their ever coming to rights. So we may expect it should be before the beginning of the glorious times of the church of God; and after this confusion, light will be the first thing that will appear. Light, clearly to explain and defend the truth and the doctrines of the Gospel, will begin to shine forth with clear and irresistible light. This lower world being without form and void at first was an image of what it was afterwards to be, a world of confusion and emptiness, vanity of vanities. (See [Notes on the] Scriptures, No. 342.[8])

73. The way of a cat with a mouse that it has taken captive is a lively emblem of the way of the Devil with many wicked men. A

mouse is a foul, unclean creature, a fit type of a wicked man, Lev. 11.29: These also shall be unclean, the weasel and the mouse; Isa. 66.17: Eating swine's flesh and the abomination and the mouse. The cat makes a play and sport of the poor mouse; so the Devil does, as it were, make himself sport with a wicked man. The cat lets the mouse go, and it seems to have escaped; it hopes it is delivered, but is suddenly catched up again before it can get clear. And so time after time, the mouse makes many vain attempts, thinks itself free when it is still a captive, is taken up again by the jaws and into the jaws of its devourer as if it were just going to be destroyed, but then is let go again, but never quite escapes, till at last it yields its life to its enemy, and is crushed between his teeth and totally devoured. So many wicked men, especially false professors of religion and sinners under Gospel light, are led captive by Satan at his will, are under the power and dominion of their lusts, and though they have many struggles of conscience about their sins, yet never wholly escape them. When they seem to escape, they fall into them again, and so again and again, till at length they are totally and utterly devoured by Satan.

74. Lightning more commonly strikes high things, such as high towers, spires, and pinnacles, and high trees, and is observed to be most terrible in mountainous places, which may signifie that heaven is an enemy to all proud persons and that [He] especially makes such the marks of His vengeance, Isa. 2.12–15: For the day of the Lord shall be upon every one that is proud and lofty, and upon every one that is lifted up, and he shall be brought low; and upon all the cedars of Lebanon, that are high and lifted up, and upon all the oaks of Bashan, and upon all the high mountains, and upon all the hills that are lifted up, and upon every high tower.

75. That balm that came chiefly from Gilead, that was used in the land of Israel and in all those eastern parts of the world, and so is to this day, as the chief and most sovereign medicine for healing wounds, was procured by piercing the balsam-tree, whereby

the tree is caused to bleed and this blood of the tree is the balm, which if done with iron nails, the tree dies. (See Chambers.) So the blood of Christ, the sovereign balm for healing the wounds of our souls, is procured by piercing of Christ.

76. Concerning the moon and her revolution and changes, and especially conjunction with the sun, see notes on Num. 10. Concerning eclipse of the sun and moon, see notes on Scripture, No. 315.

"Notes on the Scriptures," Num. 10.10, No. 315: Concerning the festival of the new moon.

The change of the moon at her conjunction with the sun, seems to be a type of three things:

1. Of the resurrection of the church from the dead by virtue of her union with Christ, and at the coming of Christ; for the moon at her change, that lost all her light, and was extinct, and seemed to die, revives again after her conjunction with the sun.

2. Of the conversion of every believing soul, which is its spiritual resurrection. The soul in its conversion comes to Christ and closes with Christ, as the moon comes to the sun into a conjunction with him. The soul in conversion dies to sin and to the world, crucifies the flesh with the affections and lusts, dies as to its own worthiness or righteousness, whereby it is said in Scripture to be dead to the law, that it may receive new life, as the former light of the moon is extinct at its conjunction with the sun that it may receive new light. In order to our coming to Christ aright, we must not come with our own brightness, or happiness, but as stripped of all our glory, empty of all good, wholly dark, sinful, destitute, and miserable, as the moon is wholly divested of all her light at her conjunction with the sun. We must come to Christ as wholly sinful and miserable, as the moon comes to the sun in total darkness. The moon as it comes nearer the sun, grows darker and darker; so the soul, the more it is fitted for Christ, is more and more emptied of itself that it may be filled with Christ. The moon grows darker and darker in her approach to the sun; so the soul sees more and more of its own sinfulness, and vileness and misery, that it may be swallowed up in the rays of the sun of righteousness.

3. The change of the moon at her conjunction with the sun signifies

the change of the state and administration of the church at the coming of Christ.

The sun is sometimes eclipsed in his conjunction with the moon, which signifies two things, viz.:

1. The veiling of his glory by his incarnation; for as the sun has his light veiled by his conjunction with the moon in its darkness, so Christ had his glory veiled by his conjunction or union with our nature in its low and broken state: as the moon proves a veil to hide the glory of the sun, so the flesh of Christ was a veil that hid his divine glory.

2. It signifies his death. The sun is sometimes totally eclipsed by the moon at her change; so Christ died at the time of the change of the church, from the old dispensation to the new. The sun is eclipsed at his conjunction with the moon in her darkness; so Christ taking our nature upon him in his low and broken state died in it. Christ assumed his church and people, in their guilt and misery, and in their condemned, cursed, dying state, into a very close union with him, so as to become one with him; and hereby he takes their guilt on himself, and becomes subject to their sin, their curse, their death, yea, is made a curse for them; as the sun, as it were, assumes the moon in her total darkness into a close union with himself, so as to become one with her: they become concentrated, and become as it were one body circumscribed by the same circumference. And thereby he takes her darkness on himself, and becomes himself dark with her darkness, and is extinct in his union with her. The moon that receives all her light from the sun eclipses the sun, and takes away his light; so Christ was put to death by those that he came to save; he is put to death by the iniquities of those that he came to give life to, and he was immediately crucified by the hands of some of them, and all of them have pierced him in the disposition and tendency of that sin that they have been guilty of; for all have manifested and expressed a mortal enmity against him. It is an argument that the eclipse of the sun is a type of Christ's death, because the sun suffered a total eclipse miraculously at that time that Christ died.

The sun can be in a total eclipse but a very little while, much less than the moon, though neither of them can always be in an eclipse; so Christ could not, by reason of his divine glory and worthiness, be long held of death, in no measure so long as the saints may be, though it is not possible that either of them should always be held of it.

The sun's coming out of his eclipse is a figure of Christ's resurrection from the dead. As the sun is restored to light, so the moon that eclipsed him begins to receive light from him, and so to partake of his restored light. So the church, for whose sins Christ died and who has pierced Christ, rises with Christ, is begotten again to a living hope by the resurrection of Christ from the dead, is made partaker of the life and power of his resurrection, and of the glory of his exaltation, is raised up together, and made to sit together in heavenly places in him. They live, yet not they but Christ lives in them, and they are married to him that is risen from the dead. God having raised Christ, Christ quickens them who were totally dark and dead in trespasses and sins, and they are revived by God's power, according to the exceeding greatness of His power that wrought in Christ Jesus, when He raised him from the dead.

The moon is eclipsed when at its full, in its greatest glory, which may signify several things:

1. That God is wont to bring some great calamity on His visible church, when in its greatest glory and prosperity, as He did in the Old Testament church, in the height of its glory, in David and Solomon's times, by David's adultery and murder, and those sore calamities that followed in his family, and to all Israel in the affairs of Amnon, and especially Absalom, and in the idolatry of Solomon and the sore calamities that followed, and particularly the dividing the kingdom of Israel. So He did also on the church of the New Testament after Constantine, by the Arian heresy, etc. God doth thus to stain the pride of all glory, and that His people may not lift up themselves against Him, that He alone may be exalted.

2. That it is often God's manner to bring some grievous calamity on his saints, at times when they have received the greatest light and joys, and have been most exalted with smiles of heaven upon them; as Jacob was made lame at the same time that he was admitted to so extraordinary a privilege as wrestling with God, and overcoming Him, and so obtaining the blessing. And so Paul, when he was received up to the third heaven, received a thorn in the flesh, lest he should be exalted above the measure; he had a messenger of Satan to buffet him. So grievous calamity it was that he laboured under, that he besought the Lord thrice that it might be taken from him. Sometimes extraordinary light and comfort is given to fit for great calamities, and sometimes for death, which God brings soon after such things; so when God gives His own people great temporal prosperity, He is wont to bring with it some calamity to eclipse it, to keep them from being exalted in their prosperity and trusting in it.

77. There is a wonderfull analogy between what is seen in RIVERS, their gathering from innumerable small branches beginning at a great distance one from another in different regions, some on the sides or tops of mountains, others in valleys, and all conspiring to one common issue, all after those very diverse and contrary courses which they held for a while, yet all gathering more and more together the nearer they come to their common end and ultimate issue, and all at length discharging themselves at one mouth into the same ocean. Here is livelily represented how all things tend to one, even to God, the boundless ocean, which they can add nothing to, as mightiest rivers that continually discharge themselves into the ocean add nothing to it sensibly; the waters of the ocean are not raised by it, yea, all the rivers together, great and small, together with all the brooks and little streams, can't raise the waters of the ocean in the least degree. The innumerable streams of which great rivers are constituted, running in such infinitely various and contrary courses, livelily represent the various dispensations of divine providence: some of them beginning at the greatest distance from the common mouth, others nearer to it, multitudes of them meeting first to constitute certain main branches of the river before they empty themselves into the main river and so into the ocean; some of the first constituent streams never empty themselves into any of the branches at all, but empty themselves directly into the main river; others first empty themselves into other branches, and those into others, and those still into others, and so on many times before they yield their tribute to the main river; several springs first constitute a brook, and then many of these brooks constitute a small river, and then several of these small rivers meet to constitute a main branch of the main river, and then all together empty into that main river. Some of the constituent branches of the main river have their head or source at the greatest distance from the mouth, others take their source much nearer the mouth, and so all along there are new heads or new sources beginning, from the head to the mouth of the main river. Some of these branches run directly contrary to others, and yet all meet at last. And the same branches don't

keep the same course: their course is not continually in a right line, that which appears to us the directest course to the main river, but sometimes they run one way, sometimes another, sometimes their course is directly contrary to what it is at others. Sometimes, instead of going towards the main river they tend to, they run for a considerable space right from it, but yet nothing is lost by this, but something gained; they nevertheless fail not of emptying themselves into the main river in proper time and due place, and bring the greater tribute of waters for their crooked and contrary courses. And so it is with the main river itself: its course is not directly the shortest way towards the ocean to which its waters are due, but tends thither by degrees, with many windings and turnings, sometimes seeming to run from the ocean and not towards it. If a spectatour were to judge by the appearances of things before his eyes, he would think the river could [not] reach the ocean. There appears such an innumerable multitude of obstacles in the way, many hills and high mountains, which a person that views at a distance sees no way between; he don't discover those ways through the hideous forests, and the openings between the mountains are not to be seen till we come to them, the winding passages through mountainous country are not to be discovered but by tracing the course of the waters themselves, but yet amidst all these obstacles those rivers find their way, and fail not at last of an arrival at the ocean at last, though they pass through so many vast regions, that all seem to be full of obstacles for so long a course together. And it is observable that those very hills and mountains that appear like the most unsurmountable obstacles, instead of obstructing the course of these rivers, do afford the greatest supplies and additions. Those rivers will at last come to the ocean, and it is impossible to hinder. It is in vain for men to attempt to turn back the stream or put a stay to it. Whatever obstacles are in the way, the waters will either bear them away before them or will find a passage round them, under them, or above them. I need not run the parallel between this and the course of God's providence through all ages from the beginning to the end of the world, when all things shall have their final issue in God, the infinite, inextinguishable fountain whence all things come at first as all the rivers come from the sea and whither they all shall come at last. For of Him and to Him are all things, and He is the alpha and omega, the beginning and the end. God hath provided a water course for the overflowing of the waters, and He turns the rivers of water whithersoever it pleaseth Him.

By what has been spoken of, it is particularly livelily represented and shown after what manner all the dispensations of providence, from the beginning of the world till the coming of Christ, all pointed to Christ, all had respect to his coming and working our redemption and setting up his kingdom in the world, and all finally issued in this great event. From time to time, in the different successive ages of the world, there began new dispensations of providence, tending to make way and forward this great event, as there are head[s] of new branches all along as we come nearer and nearer to the mouth of the main river. Thus in Noah began a new series of dispensations of providence in addition to what had been begun before, making further preparation for the coming of the Messiah. Again, in Abraham began another remarkeable course of providences to make way for the same event, which held till Christ came. So again in the redemption out of Egypt, and in David, and in the Babylonish captivity. The course of divine providence seems to be represented by a river in Gen. 41.1, 3, and Ezek. 1.1. It was over a river that Ezekiel saw the wheels of providence, so verse 3; so again Dan. 8.2, 3, 16, and Dan. 10.4, 5, and 12.6–8. (See the next.)

78. (See the last.) We see the reverse in TREES from what we do in [rivers]. In these, all comes from one common stock and is distributed into innumerable branches, beginning at the root where the trunk is biggest of all and ending in the extremities of the smallest twigs. The water here in the sap of these trees has a contrary course from what it has in rivers, where the course begins in the extremities of the smallest branches and ends in the mouth of the river where the river is largest, and all the waters are collected into one body. What is observable in trees is also a

lively emblem of many spiritual things, as particularly of the dispensations of providence since the coming of Christ. Christ is, as it were, the trunk of the tree, and all the church are his branches. I am the vine, ye are the branches, says Christ. Christ rising from the dead is, as it were, the trunk of the tree which appears coming out of the ground, and how do we from this one rising head see the body of Christ multiplied. The Christian church, as distinguished from the Jewish, began in Christ's resurrection, and how many branches shot forth soon after Christ's resurrection: the apostles after that were endowed with power from on high; those were, as it were, main branches, whence all the lesser branches came. The Apostle Paul, who was a branch that shot forth later than the rest, exceeded all in thriftiness and fruitfullness, so that the bigger part of the future tree came from this branch. The tree went on growing, and the further it proceeded in its growth, the more abundantly did its branches multiply, till the tree filled the Roman Empire in a few hundreds of years, and will fill the whole earth at last. Thus the parable of the grain of mustardseed is verified. This tree will appear more and more glorious, till it shall appear in the greatest glory of all at the end of all things, and its full ripe fruits shall be gathered in, and though there have been many winters and may be more, wherein this tree has ceased growing and has been in a great measure stripped of leaves and fruit, and seemed to be dead or dying, yet springs and summers are appointed to follow these winters, wherein the tree shall flourish again and appear higher and larger and more abundantly multiplied in its branches and fruit than ever before. This tree is sometimes represented as first beginning in Abraham, and sometimes in David, and Christ himself as the branch of those roots, but Christ is most properly the trunk or body of the tree. Indeed, the course of the sap of the tree, from its beginning in the extremities of the roots to its end in the extremity of the branches, is an emblem of the whole series and scheme of divine providence, both before and after Christ, from the beginning to the end of the world. The sap in the roots is like the water of a river gathering from small branches into a common body, and this, as was said before, represents the course of divine providence during the times of the Old Testament, when the designs of providence as they related to Christ and the work of redemption, which is as it were the summary comprehension of all God's works of providence, was hid as it were underground. All was under a veil and the scheme of redemption was a mystery kept secret from the foundation of the world; but after this, the mystery was removed, and the scheme of providence was, like a tree above ground, gradually displayed as the branches successively put forth themselves. Hence we may observe that God's calling of Abraham and anointing David was, as it were, the planting the root whence the tree should grow, and Abraham and David were main roots whence the tree grows, but Christ himself is the sprout or branch from these roots which becomes the tree whence all other branches proceed.

79. The whole material universe is preserved by gravity or attraction, or the mutual tendency of all bodies to each other. One part of the universe is hereby made beneficial to another; the beauty, harmony, and order, regular progress, life, and motion, and in short all the well-being of the whole frame depends on it. This is a type of love or charity in the spiritual world.

80. When the sun sets in red, it is a sign that it will bring a fair day when it rises. So Christ the sun of righteousness set in blood. The sun is a type of Christ, his setting is a type of his death, which was with blood and dreadfull sufferings, and thereby rose with a fair day. By this means he rose, without clouds, in clear light, blessedness, and honour, for himself and all on whom he shines.

81. The Roman triumph was a remarkeable type of Christ's ascension. The general of the Roman armies was sent forth from Rome, that glorious city and metropolis of the world, by the supream Roman authority into remote parts and the enemies' country, to fight with the enemies of the Roman state: as Christ, the captain of the Lord's hosts, was sent forth from heaven, the head city of

the universe, by the supream authority of heaven, into the remote country, the country of heaven's enemies, to conflict with those enemies. And on obtaining some very signal and great victory he returned in triumph to the city whence he came out, entered the city in a very glorious manner. So Christ, having gone through the terrible conflict and obtained a compleat and glorious victory, returned again to heaven, the city whence he came, in a glorious, triumphant manner. When the authority of Rome heard of his victory, they sent him the title of Imperator. So when Christ had conquered his enemies, he was invested with the greatest honour of rule and command; all power was given him in heaven and on earth. As the Roman general was coming towards the city of Rome, the Roman people and even the senate themselves went forth to meet him and marched in order before him to the Capitol, the principal building of the whole city, wherein was their chief temple of Jupiter and where was the place of the sitting of the senate. So when Christ was ascending to heaven, the inhabitants of heaven came forth to meet him, even the most glorious angels and archangels, the nobles and princes of that city, and joyfully conducted him to the highest and most honourable part of that city. The Roman general was richly clad in a purple robe embroidered with figures of gold setting forth his glorious achievements; his buskins were set with pearl, he wore a crown of laurel or of gold, which livelily represents the glory of Christ's ascension when he came from the slaughter of his enemies, red in his apparel, travelling in the greatness of his strength and glorious in his apparel, Isa. 63.1. He was drawn in a chariot adorned with ivory and plates of gold. So Christ is represented as ascending in the chariots of God after glorious victories over his enemies, Ps. 68.17, 18: The chariots of God are twenty thousand, even thousands of angels, the Lord is among them as in Sinai, his holy place; Thou·hast ascended on high (together with other parts of the Psalm). At the feet of the triumphing general were his children. So Christ, when he ascended into glory, did as it were carry up with him his children. He went into glory and took possession of it as their head, and not only for himself but also for them, and actually carried a number of them with him, and at his second ascension, after the day of judgment, will carry all of them with him. The cavalcade was led up by musicians. So God went up with a shout, and the most high with the sound of a trumpet. Christ's ascension was attended with the joyfull and glorious praises and songs of the heavenly hosts, represented by the joyfull musick and songs that attended the carrying up the ark into Mt. Sinai and the hosannas that attended Christ's entry into Jerusalem. And as then they strewed their garments in the way, and cut down branches of palm trees and strewed them in the way, singing praises to him as he passed, so before the triumphal chariot as it passed they all along strewed flowers, the musick playing in praise of the conquerour amidst the loud acclamations of the people crying, Io triumphe. The cavalcade was followed by the spoils taken from the enemy, their horses, arms, gold, silver, machines, tents, etc.; after these came the kings, princes or generals subdued, loaden with chains and followed by mimicks and buffoons, who insulted over their misfortunes, which is very agreeable to what is said of Christ with an evident allusion to the Roman triumphs in Colos-[sians] 2.15: And having spoiled principalities and powers, he made a shew of them openly, triumphing over them in it. Next came the officers of the conquering troops, with crowns on their heads. So the disciples of Christ, especially those that have had the greatest share with Christ in his conflicts, such as the holy martyrs and those that Christ has improved as the chief ministers of his kingdom, shall triumph with him, and be crowned and glorified together, and shall reign with him. The triumphal chariot was followed by the senate clad in white robes, and the senate by such citizens as had been set at liberty or ransomed, as Christ in his triumph is attended by the glorious angels, principalities, and powers in heavenly places, together with those saints, citizens of heaven, that have been ransomed and set at liberty by Christ, and these all as it were clothed with white robes. (Rev. 19.13, 14, and 7.9, and 3.5, 18, and 6.11.) The procession in the Roman triumphs was closed by the sacrifices, and their officers and utensils, with a white ox led along for the chief victim. In this order they proceeded through the triumphal gate, along the Via Sacra, to the Capitol, where the victims were offered; in the mean time all the temples were open, and all the altars loaden with offerings and incense, which represent Christ at his ascension entering into the holiest of all with his own blood, with his sufficient and perfect sacrifice, and the abundant incense of his mouth, to present them there to God, the consequence of which is the abundant opening the temple of God to the giving free access to all. Those Roman triumphs were attended with games in publick places and rejoicings every where, representing the unspeakable joy there was in heaven on occasion of Christ's ascension, which was attended with the utter confusion of Christ's enemies and their entire overthrow. As in the Roman triumphs, the captives, when arrived at the Forum, were led back to prison and strangled; the rites and sacrifices being over, the triumpher treated the people in the Capitol, as Christ, when he ascended on high, received gifts for men. (See notes on Ps. 68 concerning the removal of the ark, Scripture No. 319.[9])

82. There are three sorts of inhabitants of this world inhabiting its three regions, viz., the inhabitants of the earth, and the animals that inhabit the waters under the earth, and the fowls of heaven that inhabit the air or firmament of heaven. In these is some faint shadow of the three different sorts of inhabitants of the three worlds, viz., earth, heaven, and hell. The birds represent the inhabitants of heaven. These appear beautifull above the beasts and fishes; many of them are decked with glorious colours, whereas others do but go on the earth or move in the waters. These fly with wings and are above all kinds of animals, employ themselves in musick, many of them as it were sweetly praising their creatour. The fishes in the waters under the earth represent the inhabitants of hell. The waters in Scripture is represented as the place of the dead, the Rephaim, the destroyers; and whales and sea monsters that swim in the great deep are used in Scripture as emblems of devils and the wrath of God,

and the miseries of death and God's wrath are there compared to the sea, to the deeps, to floods and billows and the like.

83. The sun makes plants to flourish when it shines after rain; otherwise it makes them wither. So clouds and darkness and rains of affliction fit the soul for the clear shining of the sun of righteousness. Light and comfort of the heart, if not prepared by humiliation, do but make the heart worse; they fill it with the disease of pride and destroy the wellfare of the soul instead of promoting it. (II Sam. 23.4.)

84. The torrents and floods of liquid fire that sometimes are vomited out from the lower parts of the earth, the belly of hell, by the mouths of volcanos, indicate or shadow forth what is in hell, viz., as it were, a lake of fire and brimstone, deluges of fire and wrath to overwhelm wicked men, and mighty cataracts of wrath to come pouring down out of heaven on the heads of wicked men, as mighty torrents of liquid fire have sometimes come pouring down from Mount Etna and Vesuvius on cities or villages below. Such things do forebode the general conflagration.

85. Concerning the rising of the sun, see notes on Ps. 19.4, 5, 6, Scripture No. 328.

"Notes on the Scriptures," Ps. 19.4–6, No. 328: It appears to me very likely that the Holy Ghost in these expressions which he most immediately uses about the rising of the sun has an eye to the rising of the sun of righteousness from the grave, and that the expressions that the Holy Ghost here uses are conformed to such a view. The times of the Old Testament are times of night in comparison of the Gospel day and are so represented in Scripture, and therefore the approach of the day of the New Testament dispensation in the birth of Christ is called the day spring from on high visiting the earth. . . . But this Gospel dispensation commences with the resurrection of Christ. Therein the sun of righteousness rises from under the earth as the sun appears to do in the morning and comes forth as a bridegroom. . . .

He that was covered with contempt, and overwhelmed in a deluge of sorrow, hath purchased and won his spouse (for he loved the church and gave himself for it, that he might perfect it to himself); now he comes forth as a bridegroom to bring home his purchased spouse to him in spiritual marriage, as he soon after did in the conversion of such multitudes, making his people willing in the day of his power, and hath also done many times since, and will do in a yet more glorious degree. And as the sun when it rises comes forth like a bridegroom gloriously adorned, so Christ in his resurrection entered on his state of glory. After his state of sufferings, he rose to shine forth in ineffable glory as the king of heaven and earth, that he might be a glorious bridegroom in whom his church might be unspeakably happy.

Here the psalmist says that God has placed a tabernacle for the sun in the heavens, so God the Father had prepared an abode in heaven for Jesus Christ; He had set a throne for him there, to which he ascended after he rose. The sun after it is risen ascends up to the midst of heaven, and then at that end of its race, descends again to the earth; so Christ when he rose from the grave ascended up to the height of heaven and far above all heavens, but at the end of the Gospel-day will descend again to the earth.

It is here said that the risen sun rejoiceth as a strong man to run his race. So Christ when he rose, rose as a man of war, as the Lord strong and mighty, the Lord mighty in battle; he rose to conquer his enemies, and to show forth his glorious power in subduing all things to himself, during that race which he had run, which is from his resurrection to the end of the world, when he will return to the earth again. . . .

That the Holy Ghost here has a mystical meaning, and has respect to the light of the sun of righteousness, and not merely the light of the natural sun, is confirmed by the verse that follows, in which the psalmist himself seems to apply them to the word of God, which is the light of that sun, even of Jesus Christ, who himself revealed the word of God. See the very next words: The law of the Lord is perfect, converting the soul; the testimony of the Lord is sure, making wise the simple.

86. As it is in the analogy there is to be observed in the workes of nature, wherein the inferiour are images of the superiour, and the analogy holds through many ranks of beings, but be-

comes more and more faint and languid. Thus how many things in brutes are analagous to what is to be observed in men: in some the image is more lively, in others less, till we come to the lowest rank of brutes, in whom it is more faint than others. But if we go from them to plants, still the analogy and similitude holds in many things and in different degrees in different plants, till we come to metals and some other inanimate things, wherein still is to be seen some very faint represent[ations] of things appertaining to mankind. So it is with respect to the representations there are in the external world of things in the spiritual world. Thus the visible heavens are a type of the highest heavens, but in a lower degree mountains are types of heaven. The great deep under the earth is a type of hell, but in a lesser degree valleys and the water that is in vallies is so. The stars are types of saints in glory, and in a fainter degree the singing birds that fly in the firmament of heaven are so. And so in innumerable instances, and the same is to be observed of the types of Scripture.

87. He that is bitten with a poisonous serpent is exceedingly inclined to sleep, and is averse to a being kept awake; but if he sleeps in such circumstances, it is very mortal to him. So it is with respect to those that are bitten with the old serpent, the Devil.

88. Multitudes of things, when they are good for nothing else, are good to be burnt, and that is the use men put them to. So it is said of barren branches, John 15.6: They are cast forth, and men gather them and cast them into the fire, and they are burned. It is the way men dispose of useless refuse timbers of barren trees, briars and thorns, and bushes in clearing of land. So it is in spirituals.

89. It is because the providence of God is like a wheel, or a machine composed of wheels, having wheels in the midst of wheels, that it is so ordered, in the constitution of nature and

in the dispositions of God's providence, that almost all the curious machines that men contrive, to do any notable things or produce any remarkeable effect, are by wheels, a compage of wheels, revolving round and round, going and returning, representing the manner of the progress of things in divine providence.

90. A corn of wheat is sown, then arises and flourishes considerably, but before it rises to its height, before the perfect plant arises or the proper and perfect fruit produced, a long winter comes upon it and stunds it, and then, when those many days of severe cold and frost are past, when the spring comes on, it revives and flourishes far beyond what it did before and comes to its height a perfect plant. Then comes the harvest. So is it with Christ: he was slain and arose, and his church flourished glorious in the days of the apostles, and afterwards then succeeded those many days of affliction, persecution, and darkness and deadness. But we know the spring is coming.

91. The constitution of the Roman polity which flourished in the time of Christ and his apostles was in many respects a lively image of the constitution of the spiritual polity of the heavenly Jerusalem or the church of Christ, and among other things in this: that there were many that were called and treated as Roman citizens that were free of the city and enjoyed the priviledges of the city and were looked upon as properly belonging to that city, that dwelt in other cities, at a great distance from Rome, yea, and never saw Rome. So many properly belong to the heavenly; they have their citizenship in heaven that hitherto dwelt at a great distance from heaven and never as yet have been in heaven but dwelt here in another country.

92. How much favour and esteem is undoing them daily in everything, and how much of a moral does this carry in it! [10]

93. Blue that is the colour of the skie fades not, intimating that the beauty and lustre of heavenly things is unfading.

94. A gathering time or harvest is succeeded by a threshing and winnowing to separate the wheat from the straw and chaff, and grinding and sifting to separate from the bran. So many trials and afflictions are wont to follow the elects' being brought home to Christ, to separate between them and their remaining corruptions, and particularly very commonly a time of great persecution very commonly follows a remarkeable harvest in the church of God. So it was after that great ingathering soon after Christ's ascension, and so it was after that great ingathering at the Reformation. Hence Christ compares the trials of the godly to the sifting of wheat. (Luke 22.31.)

95. That place in Genesis, Upon thy belly shalt thou go and dust shalt thou eat, as it undoubtedly in part has respect to the manner of the serpent's going, which is by crawling on his belly, so it shews that that manner of going of the serpent was so ordered on purpose (partly at least) to be a representation of some curse inflicted on the Devil, who undoubtedly is the principal subject of the curse here denounced, and therefore it proves that outward things are ordered as they be to that end, that they might be images of spiritual things.

96. The heat of the sun in summer is to many things as trials and sufferings are to the souls of professours of godliness. It dries up the puddles of snow water; though for a while they seem to run very freely, they dry up because they have no fountains sufficient for their supply, they are not fed by living springs. So those herbs and plants that have no deepness of earth, they wither away. So many fruits, though they blossom in the spring, looked as firm as any and the fruit seemed at first to be promising, yet as the heat of the summer comes on, they wither up, whereas the more sound fruits receive no damage

by this heat, but are rather better and brought to that proper ripeness and perfection by it.

97. The beams of the sun can't be scattered, nor the constant stream of their light in the least interrupted or disturbed by the most violent winds here below, which is a lively image of what is true concerning heavenly light communicated from Christ, the sun of righteousness, to the soul. It is not in the power of the storms and changes of the world to destroy that light and comfort. Yea, death itself can have no hold of it. The reasons why the sunlight is not disturbed by winds is twofold: 1. the light is of so pure and subtle a nature that that which is so gross as the wind can have no hold of it; and 2. the sun, the luminary, is far above, out of the reach of winds. Those things are lively images of what is spiritual.

98. Man is made with his feet on the earth and with his posture erect and countenance towards heaven, signifying that he was made to have heaven in his eye and the earth under foot. (See Mr. Henry on Gen. 1.1; [11] see Image 133.)

99. A tree that has so many branches from one stock and root, from so small a seed and a little twig, that gradually increases more and more becomes so great in so manifold branches, twigs, leaves, flowers, fruit, appearing so beautifull and flourishing under the light of the sun and influences of the rain, is a lively image of the church of God, which is often compared to it in the Scripture. It is represented by an olive tree and vine and a palm tree, and the bush on Mt. Sinai, trees of lign-aloes, cedar tree, etc. The church in different ages is lively represented by the growth and progress of a tree, and the church in the pure age in Christ, its head and stock, is like a tree. The various changes of a tree in different seasons, and what comes to pass in its leaves, flowers, and fruit, innumerable instances that might be mentioned, is a lively image of what is to be seen in the church. The ingrafting of a tree, and the various things done about it

by the husbandman, also represent what is to be seen in the church. There is a marvellous representation of the abundant profusion of God's goodness and lovely grace in what is to be seen in a tree, therein representing what is to be seen in the church. Some particular sorts of trees do more represent the church in some accounts, and others in others, as the vine, the olive, the palm, the apple tree, etc. A tree also is many ways a lively image of a particular Christian with regard to the new man, and is so spoken of in Scripture.

Corol[lary]: Hence it may be argued that infants do belong to the church.

100. By the vicissitudes of day and night in this world God teaches that we are to expect changes here and must not expect always to enjoy a sunshine of prosperity, but must have a vicissitude and mixture of prosperity and adversity.

101. Olympick games: see Turrentine, Vol. 2, p. 546 at top.[12]

102. Grasshoppers and other insects that are idle and don't lay up food in summer against winter, as the ant and bee does, but spend the time in singing, are never so brisk asinging as on the approach of winter, or just before they are destroyed by the frost, which represents what is spoken of in Matt. 24.37: But as it was in the days of Noah, etc. (See Image 136.)

103. God shortens the night or time of darkness by the refraction of the atmosphere. So the sun is longer before it sets and sooner in rising than other wise it would be, and partly by the refraction of the atmosphere in the morning and evening twilight, so that we have less darkness than light through the year, which represents God's shortening the days of tribulation for the sake of His church. So God gives light in the time of darkness by the moon and stars, which represents those diverse sparks God gives his people in the day of their troubles so that they shall not be in total darkness or be utterly cast down, but shall have

many cordials and comforts, light sufficient to guide and divert them in what is absolutely necessary. They shall have comfort from innumerable promises and dispensations of God's word, as from so many stars, and shall have great comfort in God's ordinances in his church, which is the antitype of the light of the moon.

104. There is the tongue and another member of the body that have a natural bridle, which is to signify to us the peculiar need we have to bridle and restrain those two members.

105. When men stand on very high things they are ready to grow giddy and are in greatest danger of falling, and the higher they are the more dreadfull is their fall. Especially are those in great danger that are not used to be on high things, which represents the danger men are in when lifted up on high on the pinnacle of honour and prosperity, of having their eyes dazzle, of being very discomposed and erroneous in their notions of things, especially themselves and their own standing and the great danger they are in of falling; and how that those that are most highly exalted in pride have the most dreadfull fall.

106. If a building be built very high it must have its foundation laid answerably deep and low and must have its lower part answerably great and broad, or else it will be in danger of falling. So if a man be lifted up high in honour and prosperity, he will be in great danger of being overset unless his foundation be answerably strong and his heart be answerably established in knowledge and faith, etc., and unless his lower parts, his humility, be answerably great and his foundation be laid answerably low and deep in self-abasement. The same thing is represented by this: if a ship has great sails, much of that which is displayed in the air and lifted up on high, it must have ballast answerable to sink it answerably deep. Otherwise it will be in danger of being overset.

107. That high towers and other high things are commonly smitten with thunder, and mountainous places more subject to terrible thunder and lightning, shews how that pride and self-exaltation does peculiarly excite God's wrath. (See Isa. 2.17, etc.)

108. Bread-corn is much used in Scripture to represent the saints. The wicked are represented by the clusters of the vine, but the godly by bread-corn. They are called Christ's wheat that he will gather into his barn and into his garner, and we are all said to be that one bread. Now this is remarkeable of wheat and other bread-corn, that it is sown and grows before winter, and then is as it were killed and long lies dead in the winter season, and then revives in the spring and grows much taller than before, and comes to perfection and brings forth fruit, which is a lively image of the resurrection of saints, as well as the grain's being first buried in the earth and dying there before it comes up. And that often comes to pass concerning the saints in this life that is livelily represented by it: after their conversion they have a falling away and long continue in a cold and dead carnal state and then revive again and grow much taller than before and never fail again till they bring fruit to perfection. It is also a lively image of what comes to pass with respect to the Christian church, which, after it was planted by the apostles and flourished a while, then fell under a wintry season, a low and very suffering state for a long while, and so continues till about the time of the destruction of antichrist, and then revives and grows and comes to a glorious degree of prosperity and fruitfullness, which is what is called in Scripture the first resurrection. Therefore it is said of Israel, Hosea 14.7: They shall revive as the corn. The reviving of the church, after a low state and a time of trouble, is compared to the reviving of corn from under the earth in the spring in Isa. 37.30, 31.

109. The inside of the body of man is full of filthiness, contains his bowels that are full of dung, which represents the corruption

and filthiness that the heart of man is naturally full of. (See
Image 145.)

110. The awaking and crowing of the cock to wake men out of
sleep and to introduce the day seems to signifie the introducing
the glorious day of the church by ministers preaching the Gospel.
Many shall be awakened and roused to preach the Gospel with
extraordinary fervency, to cry aloud and lift up their voice like
[a] trumpet. Peter's being awakened out of that deep sleep he
had fallen into, and brought to repentance by the crowing of the
cock at break of day, signifies the awakening of Christ's church
that is built upon Peter, the rousing of the wise virgins out of
that dull slumbering and backsliding state, in many respects
denying their Lord, and bringing them to repentance by the
preaching of the Gospel to introduce the morning of the glorious
times.

The introducing of the spring by the voice of spring birds
signifies the same thing.

111. The morning of the day and the spring of the year are
remarkeable types of the commencement of the glorious times
of the church. (See note on Job 38.13; see also Cant. 2.11,
etc.)

"Notes on the Scriptures," Job 38.13: That the wicked might be
shaken out of it: It is probable that one reason why God says this of the
morning is because He has in His eye that glorious morning of the light
and prosperity of the Christian church when the son of righteousness
shall arise with victory in his wings, and God shall say to His church:
Arise, shine, for thy light is come, for the glory of the Lord is risen
upon thee, which morning will be accompanied with that earthquake
that we read of, Rev. 16.8, by which the world shall be shaken, of
which morning the sun rising of the natural day is a type.

What is said in the next verse is applicable to the morning of that
glorious day more aptly than to the morning of the natural day, for
though the face of the earth and the visible objects upon it are as it were
turned and changed and put on a beautiful form at the rising of the

natural sun, so that the sun is as it were the seal and they the clay, they stand or appear as a beautiful garment that covers the earth, yet in the morning of that glorious day of the church, when the sun of righteousness shall arise, the world of mankind, the inhabitants of the earth (which seem specially to be intended by the pronoun *they* in the verse), shall be turned or changed by the appearance of that sun much more properly as clay to the seal.

112. As corn is not fit for our use till it is threshed and ground and baked in an oven, therein representing the way in which the bread that come[s] down from heaven is fitted to nourish us, so most kinds of fruits are not fit to be eaten till they are red or till their juice is become like blood, representing the way in which the fruit of the tree of life is fitted for us, viz., by Christ's death, by his shedding his blood.

113. MILK represents the word of God from the breasts of the church, that is not only represented as a woman but of old was typified by heifers, the goats, etc. Milk by its whiteness represents the purity of the word of God; it fitly represents the word because of its sweetness and nourishing nature, and being for the saints in their present state, wherein they are children. That is, as it were, the natural food of a new creature or of the creature newly come into the world; by its whiteness and purity it represents holiness, that is the natural food and delight of the new spiritual nature, for it is this is the direct object of a spiritual relish and appetite.

114. The blue colour of the serene skie, which is a pure, pleasant colour, yet is a feeble colour: it is by a reflection of the weakest and least rays of the sun's light, hereby representing admirably not only the purity of the happiness of the saints in heaven, but that blessed humility and as it were holy pusilanimity that they are of.

115. Man's inwards are full of dung and filthiness, which is to denote what the inner man, which is often represented by various

parts of his inwards, sometimes the heart, sometimes the bowels, sometimes the belly, sometimes the veins, is full of: spiritual corruption and abomination. So, as there are many foldings and turnings in the bowels, it denotes the great and manifold intricacies, secret windings and turnings, shifts, wiles, and deceits that are in their hearts. (See Image 109; Prov. 20.27; 18.8; 26.22; 20.30; and 22.18.)

116. This world is all over dirty. Everywhere it is covered with that which tends to defile the feet of the traveller. Our streets are dirty and muddy, intimating that the world is full of that which tends to defile the soul, that worldly objects and worldly concerns and worldly company tend to pollute us.

117. The water, as I have observed elsewhere, is a type of sin or the corruption of man and of the state of misery that is the consequence of it. It is like sin in its flattering discoveries. How smooth and harmless does the water oftentimes appear, and as if it had paradise and heaven in its bosom. Thus when we stand on the banks of a lake or river, how flattering and pleasing does it oftentimes appear, as though under more pleasant and delightfull groves and bowers and even heaven itself in its clearness wrought to tempt one unaquainted with its nature to descend thither. But indeed it is all a cheat: if we should descend into it, instead of finding pleasant, delightfull groves and a garden of pleasure and heaven in its clearness, we should meet with nothing but death, a land of darkness, or darkness itself, etc. (See Prov. 5.3–6.)

118. Images of divine things. It is with many of these images as it was with the sacrifices of old: they are often repeated, whereas the antitype is continual and never comes to pass but once. Thus sleep is an image of death that is repeated every night; so the morning is the image of the resurrection; so the spring of the year is the image of the resurrection which is repeated every year. And so of many other things that might be

mentioned, they are repeated often, but the antitype is but once. The shadows are often repeated to show t[w]o things, viz., [1.] that the thing shadowed is not yet fulfilled, and 2. to signify the great importance of the antitype that we need to be so renewedly and continually put in mind of it.

119. See note on Prov. 30.15, 16.

"Notes on the Scriptures," Prov. 30.15, 16: This is said to the re-proach of worldly minded men or those whose hearts are under the power of those two daughters of the horsleech, ambition and sensuality, that they are like the grave, etc. These things were designed images and types of worldliminded men, and therefore they show how mean and hatefull they are and how dreadfull their case is upon other ac-counts. They are like the grave: they are in a state of death, their souls are like sepulcres full of dead men's bones and all uncleanness. They are like the barren [womb]: greedy, taking in, sucking up the strength of the earth, the best the world can afford, and yet bringing forth no fruit, and on whom the seed of the word is poured in vain. They are like the earth: they are earthly, vile and base in their natures, as the dirt we tread under our feet. They are like the fire, by the force of their lusts consuming all things, full of violent principles of enmity against God and man that render them dangerous and exceeding hurtfull to those that come near them.

120. Tongue. God hath fixed to it a natural bridle and fenced it in with a strong wall, as it were, even the double row of teeth, to intimate how it ought to be restrained and strongly guarded.

121. When persons lay themselves down to sleep in the night they are wont to put off their garments. So it is when persons fall into a spiritual sleep. Therefore it is said, Blessed is he that watches and keepeth his garments (i.e., by keeping them on) lest he walk naked and they see his shame. So when God's people were building Jerusalem in troublous times, they did not put off their clothes. (Neh. 4.23.)

122. Men as they are born all over filthy, proceeding out of that which is filthy and being begotten in filthiness, so they are born backward into the world, with their backs upon God and heaven and their faces to the earth and hell, representing the natural state of their hearts. (See Images 10, 25.)[13]

123. The glory of the face of the earth is the grass and green leaves and flowers. These fade away, they last but a little while and then are gone. After the spring and summer, a winter comes that wholly defaces and destroys all, and that which is most taking and pleasant, and as it were the crown of its glory, viz., the flower of the trees and the field, fades soonest. The glory of the heavens consists in its brightness, its shining lights which continue the same through winter and summer, age after age. This represents the great difference between earthly glory, riches, and pleasures, which fades as the leaves and as the grass and flower of the field, and the glory and happiness of heaven, which fadeth not away, which is agreeable to many representations in the Scripture.

124. The exceeding height of heaven above the earth, even above its highest towers or mountains, denotes the unspeakeable and inconceivable height of the happiness of heaven above all earthly happiness or glory.

125. There are many things between the young birds in a nest and a dam resembling what is between Christ and his saints. The bird shelters them; so Christ shelters his saints as a bird does her young under her wings. They [are] brought forth by the dam; so the saints are Christ's children. They are hatched by the brooding of the dam; so the soul is brought forth by the warmth and heat and brooding of Christ, by the heavenly dove, the Holy Spirit. They dwell in a nest of the dam's providing, on high out of the reach of harm, in some place of safety; so are the saints in the church. They are feeble and helpless, can neither fly nor go, which represents the infant state of the saints

in this world. The manner of the dam's feeding the young, giving every one his portion, represents the manner of Christ's feeding his saints. When the dam visits the nest, all open their mouths wide together with a cry, and that is all that they can do; so should the saints do, especially at times when Christ makes special visits to his church by his spirit. They don't open their mouths in vain. So God says, Open thy mouth wide, and I will fill [it]. The birds grow by this nourishment till they fly away into heaven to sing in the firmament; so the saints are nourished up to glory.

126. As these later ages have discovered the greatness of the heavenly bodies and their height, and the smallness of the earth in comparison of the heavens to be vastly beyond what it used to be imagined to be, so are eternal and heavenly things beyond what the church of God formerly imagined them to be.

127. Poisonous and hurtfull animals, such as serpents, spiders, incline for the most part to hide themselves or lurk in secret places: herein they are types of devils and the dupes of men.

128. As the SUN is an image of Christ upon account of its pleasant light and benefits, refreshing life-giving influences, so it is on account of its extraordinary fierce heat, it being a fire of vastly greater fierceness than any other in the visible world, whereby is represented the wrath of the Lamb. This is a very great argument of the extremity of the misery of the wicked, for doubtless the substance will be vastly beyond the shadow, as God's brightness and glory is so much beyond the brightness of the sun, His image. Thus the sun is but a shade and darkness in comparison of it; so His fierceness and wrath is vastly beyond the sun's heat.

129. That a child needs correction, and the benefit of correcting children is a type of what is true with respect to God's children.

130. The Apostle argues after such a manner from what is in the body of man to what should be in the mystical body of Christ or church of God [to] show that something further than meer illustration is intended: it shews that there is a real type or intended representation of the other. Otherwise his argument can't be so forceable from these things as his manner of speaking supposes them to be.

131. The exceeding terribleness of the lion, tyger, crocadile, and some other beasts teaches the infinite horror and amazement of those that fall a prey to the Devil.

132. The Holy Ghost intends to teach divine mysteries by the signification of persons' names that were given accidentally, i.e., without any speciall command from God or any such design in them who gave the name. This seems manifest by Heb. 7.2, to signify divine things by the constitution of the world is no mere trifling.

133. The beasts are so made that they commonly go with their heads down to the earth seeking their food with their mouths in the dust or down to the very ground. But how very different is man made from them, with his head towards heaven, which shews that the highest good of the beasts is earthly, but that man's proper happiness is heavenly. (See Image 98.)

134. The very wisest heathens seemed to be sensible that the divine being, in the formation of the natural world, designed to teach us moral lessons: so Ovid concerning the erect posture of men.[14]

135. That trees were made to represent men, see note on Deut. 20.19.

"Notes on the Scriptures," Deut. 20.19: For the tree of the field is man's life: It might have been rendered much more agreeable to the original: *for man is a tree of the field.* It was God's will that fruit-full trees should not be cut down, but only trees that yielded no fruit, because trees with respect to their barrenness or fruitfullness represented man; and therefore He would deal with them as He deals with men. This is an argument in the Law of Moses itself that its commands were given from some typical respect.

136. The destruction of the face of the earth in winter is a type of the end of the world, as is evident by the appointment of the feast of tabernacles, which was at the end of the year, just before the tempestuous season began. (See notes on the feast of tabernacles.)

"Notes on the Scriptures," Zech. 14.16–19, No. 396: The feast of tabernacles here spoken of is that glorious spiritual feast that God shall provide all nations in the last ages of the world and on the expected glorious state of the church. . . . This feast was on the seventh month of the year which was a kind of an holy sabbatical month, as the seventh day of the week was an holy day, and the seventh year an holy year, and also the year of jubilee at the end of seven times seven years. . . .

The feast of tabernacles was the last feast they had in the whole year before the face of the earth was destroyed by the winter. Probably after the feast of tabernacles was over a tempestuous season began. Fasting was now dangerous because the feast was now already past. So this feast of the church will be the last feast she shall have on earth, the last pouring out of the Spirit before this lower world is destroyed. The feast of tabernacles was kept when they had gathered in the fruits of their land, . . . and is called the feast of ingathering at the end of the year; so that great spiritual feast of the church shall [come] after God's ingathering of both His harvest and vintage spoken of, Rev. 14. It will be the time of His gathering in all His good saints before winter as it were; that is, before the destruction of the world, a time when the fruits of the earth will come to their full ripeness.

137. When we first get up in the morning, we rake open and kindle up the fire; so Christians when they awake out of a spiritual sleep new-kindle their graces.

138. It is the manner of princes to stomp on their coin their image and their name. Thus Christ speaks of Caesar's image and superscription on their pieces of money, which is a type of what God doth to His saints that are His peculiar treasure, His jewels, and that are compared to pieces of money. (Luke 15.8–10.) He stomps His image on their hearts, and writes on them His name, as is often represented in Rev[elations]. He owns them for His, He challenges them as His special property.

139. The moon, which is the highest thing that belongs to the earthly system and is the top of this lower world, and, as it were, the height and brightness and glory of it, is a lively image of earthly glory and all the good of this system: very changeable, waxing and waning, one while appearing in full splendor and soon after totally extinct, constantly rising and falling. When it is come to full glory, then it is near a declension; it continues not in the full very long, and then when it is in full brightness is the time for an eclipse. It often suffers a total eclipse at that time.[15] (See Rev. 12 at the beginning.)

140. The influences of the stars on the earth and earthly things is a type of the government which God has assigned to the angels over earthly things.

141. The breath of man is, as it were, his life, hereby shewing what man's life is, even a blast of wind that goeth away and cometh not again. To this the Scripture seems to have reference in several places, as Job 7.7: O remember that my life is wind; Ps. 78.39: He remembered that they were but flesh, a wind that passeth away, and cometh not again, alluding to the breath's going forth when a person is dying. And that thin, vanishing vapour that is in the breath, that at some seasons appears but vanishes away as it were in a moment, is a type of the very thing expressed, Jam[es] 4.14: What is your life? It is even a vapour that appeareth a little while, and then vanisheth away. While the breath con-

tinues warm the vapour appears, but when that warmth is gone
the vapour disappears. This represents how suddenly our vital
heat or warmth that maintains the life of the body will be gone,
and cold death will succeed.

142. The silk-worm is a remarkeable type of Christ. Its greatest
work is weaving something for our beautifull clothing, and it dies
in this work; it spends its life on it, it finishes it in death (as Christ
was obedient unto death, his righteousness was chiefly wrought
out in dying), and then it rises again, a worm as Christ was in his
state of humiliation, but a more glorious creature when it rises. It
leaves its web for our glorious clothing behind, and rises perfectly white, denoting the purity from imputed grace with which
he rose, as our surety, for in his resurrection he was justified.

143. The superiour heavens are much more immoveable and less
subject to change than those inferiour heavens that are nearer to
the earth, for in these the planets move and change their places,
and are unsteady in their motion, and are in themselves opake and
shine with far less brightness, and are subject to wax and wane,
some of them in their light and some of them subject to eclipses,
as the two greater lights, the sun and moon. And besides in them
appear many comets of a most unsteady motion, variable appearance, and short continuance. But in the superiour heavens the innumerable multitude of stars are all fixed immoveable, and shine
with a vastly superiour brightness, and without waxing or waning
or eclipses, representing the durableness and brightness of the
glory of the highest heavens, as a kingdom that cannot be moved,
the things of which are things that cannot be shaken.

144. As the worm's dying and remaining in aurelia state, and
then rising a glorious flying creature, represents the resurrection
of a saint, so the spots of gold that are on the aurelia represent the
preciousness of the dust of the saint, even while it remains in a
state of death, being still united to Christ, and precious to him.

145. If persons have dirt in their eyes it exceedingly hinders their sight. This represents how much it blinds men when their eyes are full of the world or full of earth. In order to the clearness of our sight we had need to have our eyes clear of earth, i.e., our aims free from all things belonging to this earthly world, and to look only at those things that are spiritual, agreeable to what Christ says: If thine eye be single, thy whole body shall be full of light, but if thine eye be evil, thy whole body shall be full of darkness.

146. The late invention of telescopes, whereby heavenly objects are brought so much nearer and made so much plainer to sight and such wonderfull discoveries have been made in the heavens, is a type and forerunner of the great increase in the knowledge of heavenly things that shall be in the approaching glorious times of the Christian church.

147. The changing of the course of trade and the supplying of the world with its treasures from America is a type and forerunner of what is approaching in spiritual things, when the world shall be supplied with spiritual treasures from America.

148. Foxes: remarkeable types of devils and other enemies of the church of God: see Mr. Hollenbrock's sermon on Cant. 2.15, from p. 4 to p. 12. See also note on Cant. 2.15.

"Notes on the Scriptures," Cant. 2.15: Take us the foxes, the little foxes that spoil the vines, for our vines have tender grapes: which represent the first sins that spoil the graces of the saints in their present imperfect state, in which their graces are like tender grapes, easily damnified. These sins that spoil the graces are represented by foxes because [of] their sly, deceitfull manner in which they insinuate themselves, and little foxes because the sins that are intended are not what are called gross sins but other sins which the saints are more incident to; or

2ndly, they represent sly deceivers who don't appear as open and declared enemies to the church, nor their wickedness so great as to be plain and manifest, and tend at first sight to shock the minds of the saints, which sly deceivers do corrupt and spoil young and tender converts in a time of great revival of religion. Such a time is spoken of in the context. (Hereby also it is signified that Christ would have sin and errour nipped in the bud, who though at first they are like young foxes, yet even they spoil the vines, and if let alone will soon grow great.) Such foxes to destroy young and tender grapes were the false prophets and seducers in the apostles' day whom the Apostle calls deceitfull workers who crept into houses and led captive silly women.

149. (Add this to Image 68.) These two things, the blood and the fat, as they were those parts of animals that were especially appropriated for sacrifices, so they were the only parts of beasts which they were forbidden to eat, and particularly the fat of the kidneys, Lev. 3.15–17: And the two kidneys and the fat that is upon them, which is by the flanks, and the caul above the liver with the kidneys, it shall be taken away; the priest shall burn them upon the altar: it is the food of the offering made by fire for a sweet savour; all the fat is the Lord's. It shall be for a perpetual statute for your generations throughout all your dwellings, *that ye eat neither fat nor blood*. And so Lev. 7.23–27. They are there forbidden to eat either of these with the greatest strictness, with awfull curses added. And therefore these being things in brute beasts that never were their food at all, but were things that they were to abominate the thoughts of eating, they were the most unlikely of any part of the animals they used for food to be made use of as metaphorical representations of their vegetable food, unless it were upon some mystical or typical consideration. If it was the design to represent their vegetable food by a metaphor taken from their animal food only for the sake of elegancy of speech, surely the metaphor would have been taken from that which was indeed some part of their animal [food] and not those parts of them only singled out which never were their food and which they were to abhor the thoughts of eating, and were forbidden on any account to eat under the pain of God's most fearfull curses.

150. It was the manner at the time that Christ appeared in the world, and in the preceding and following ages, for kings to wear robes of purple and scarlet robes, which was some representation of the apparel of him that God had appointed as king over the earth, who was in a mystical sense red in his apparel, having his garments stained first with his own blood and then with the blood of his enemies, as Isa. 63. Therefore Christ him[self] in the time of his last suffering had on him a scarlet and purple robe, which was to represent the same thing, though they that put it on meant not so.

151. (Vid. Images 29 and 67.) As one ascends a mountain, they get further and further from this lower world, and the objects of it look less and less to him. So it is in one that ascends in the way to heaven. Commonly near the foot of an high mountain there is a deep valley which must be descended in order to come to the mountain. So we must first descend low by humiliation to fit us for spiritual exaltation.

152. The changes that pass on the face of the earth by the gradual approach of the sun is a remarkeable type of what will come to pass in the visible church of God and world of mankind in the approach of the church's latter day glory. The latter will be gradual, as the former is. The light and warmth of the sun in the former is often interrupted by return of clouds and cold, and the fruits of the earth kept back from a too sudden growth and a too quick transition from the dead state in winter to their summer's glory, which in the end would be hurtfull to them and would kill them. So it is in the spiritual world: if there should be such warm weather constantly without interruption as we have sometimes in Feb., March, and April, the fruits of the earth would flourish mightily for a little while, but would not be prepared for the summer's heat, but that would kill them. This is typical of what is true concerning the church of God and particular souls. The earth being stripped of its white winter garments in which all looked clean, but all was dead, and the making of it so dirty as it is early

in the spring in order to fit it for more beautifull clothing in a living state in summer, is also typical of what passes in the spiritual change of the world and also a particular soul. The surface of the earth is, as it were, dissolved in the spring; the ground is loosened and broke up and soften[ed] with moisture, and its filthiness never so much appears as then, and then is the most windy, turbulent season of all.

153. Plutarch observes of the ass, which is of all creatures the dullest, that it has the fattest heart. Thence the expression in Scripture: Go, make their hearts fat, i.e., gross and dull.

There is a fish that they call Ονος, the ass fish, which hath its heart in its belly, a fit emblem of a sensual epicure. (See Manton on James, p. 535.[16])

154. The revolutions of the spheres of the heavens are a great representation of the revolutions of the wheels of providence. And in the system of the world, there is a wheel in the midst of a wheel, the lesser spheres within the greater making several revolutions while the greater make one; and there are the revolutions also of the satellites, that are like a lesser wheel joined to a greater, making many lesser revolutions while the greater makes one, very aptly representing the manner of things proceeding in divine providence. (See note on Ezekiel's wheels, Scripture No. 389.) The revolutions of the wheels of providence are aptly represented by the revolutions of the heavenly bodies, for they are those that rule the times and seasons, and are given for times and for seasons, and for days and for years, and hereby and by their secret influences on sublunary things, represent the angels, the ministers of God's providence. The changes of time by the revolutions of the wheels of providence are fitly represented by those heavenly bodies that God has made to be the great measurers of time by their revolutions.

"Notes on the Scriptures," Ezek. 1, No. 389: Divine providence is most aptly represented by the revolution and course of those wheels.

Things in their series and course in providence, they do as it were go round like a wheel in its motion on the earth. That which goes round like a wheel goes from a certain point or direction till it gradually returns to it again. So is the course of things in providence.

God's providence over the world consists partly in His governing the natural world according to the course and laws of nature. This consists wholly as it were in the revolution of wheels: so the annual changes that appear in the natural world are as it were by the revolution of a wheel or the course of the sun through the great circle, . . . the rising of that great wheel, the zodiach; and so the monthly changes are by the revolution of another lesser wheel within that greater annual, which being a lesser wheel must go round oftener to make the same progress. Ezekiel's vision was of wheels within wheels, of lesser wheels within greater wheels, all went round as though running upon several parallel plains, each touching the circumference of its respective wheel, and all making the same progress, keeping pace one with another; and therefore the smaller wheels must go round so much oftener, according as their circumference was less. So again, the diurnal changes in the natural world are by the revolution of a wheel still within the monthly wheel, and going round about 30 times in one revolution of the other. (Here add No. 394.)

("Notes on the Scriptures," No. 394: The system of the universe may exactly confirm what is here said of those wheels and livelily represents God's providence in the government of the moral world. There is as it were a wheel within a wheel, the whole system is nothing else but wheels within wheels, lesser wheels within greater. Revolving oftener there is the sphere of the fixed stars, which is the greatest wheel and inclines all the others, is many thousand years in performing its revolution; this includes the circle of Saturn's course which is a lesser wheel within the other, finishing its revolution in about 30 years; that includes the circle of Jupiter, a lesser wheel revolving in about 12 years; that includes the circle of Mars; that the circle of the earth, that of Venus, that of Mercury, that the sun, which revolves about its own axis. And some of the greater wheels include lesser ones of various kinds, as the great wheel of Saturn, besides those of the inferiour planets, has annexed to it those lesser wheels of his satellites, one within another, and then its ring, and then its own body about its axis; so of Jupiter, and so the earth and moon. So some of the grand revolutions of providence that are but parts of the grand system of providence have a particular system as it were belonging to themselves, wherein the great revolution includes lesser revolutions that are not parallel with any like ones continued from the beginning to the end of time, but begin their various revolutions with that particular great wheel that they are affixed to and end with it. So it is with that great wheel, the continuance of the Jewish state. So it is with the continuance of the Christian church; so it is with the state of some parts under kingdoms and empires.)

So it is with the motions of the air in the winds, it goes and returns according to its circuits; and so it is with the motion of the waters in the tides and in their course out of the sea and into the clouds, streams and rivers, and into the sea again. So it is with the circulation of the blood in a man's body and the bodies of other animals. So it is with the life of man, it is like the revolution of a wheel: he is from the earth and gradually rises, and then gradually falls and returns to the earth again. Dust we are and unto dust we return; we came naked out of our mother's womb and naked must we go, and return as we came, as it were out [of] our mother's womb; the dust returns to earth as it was and the spirit returns to God who gave it. So it is with the world of mankind: it is the whole of it like a wheel. It as it were sinks and goes down to the earth in one generation and rises in another, and as it is with a wheel, at the same time that one side is falling to the earth, another part of the wheel is rising from the earth. . . .

So it is in the course of things in God's providence over the intelligent and moral world, all is the motion of wheels. They go round and come to the same [place] again, and the whole series of divine providence from the beginning to the end is nothing else but the revolution of certain wheels, greater and lesser, the lesser being contained within the greater. What comes to pass in the natural world is in this respect typical of what comes to pass in the moral and intelligent world. . . .

Things in their series and course in providence do, as it were, return to the same point or place whence they began, as in the turning of a wheel, but yet not so but that a further end is obtained than was at first, or the same end is obtained in a much further degree. So that in the general there is a progress towards a certain fixed issue of things, and every revolution brings nearer to that issue, as it is in the motion of a wheel upon the earth or in the motion of the wheels of a chariot, and not like the motion of a wheel on its axis, for if so, its motion would be vain. . . .[17]

155. The spring season is spoken of in Scripture as representing a season of the outpouring of the spirit of God. As it is so in many other accounts, so in these. In the spring the seed that is sown in stony places sprouts and looks as fair as that in good ground, though in the summer, for want of moisture and deepness of earth, it withers away. In the spring innumerable flowers and young fruits appear flourishing and bid fair, that afterwards drop off and come to nothing. (See Misc. No. 1,000.) In the spring many streams flow high, many from snow water, though not every day even in the spring, but on warm days by fits, and are frozen up between whiles, like hypocrites' affections by pangs during a great outpouring of the spirit. And in the spring also those streams that flowed from living fountains and ran all winter and summer are greatly increased. But when the spring is over, all streams are totally dried up but those that are supplied by living springs.

So a shower of rain is like an outpouring of the spirit: it makes water flow abundantly in the streets and greatly raises streams from living fountains; and when the shower is over, the streams in the streets are dried up and the streams from living fountains are diminished. So a shower causes mushrooms suddenly to spring up, as well as good plants to grow, and blasts many fruits as well as bring[s] others to perfection. (In the spring of the year when the birds sing, the frogs and toads also croak. So at the same time that the saints sing God's praises, hypocrites sing also, but the voice is as different in God's ear as the sweet singing of birds and the croaking of toads and frogs.)

"Miscellanies," No. 1,000: Blossoms may look fair, and not only so but smell sweet, send forth pleasant odour, and yet come to nothing. It is the fruit, therefore, and neither leaves nor blossoms is that by which we must judge of the tree. So persons talk about things of religion, may appear fair and may be exceeding savoury, and the saints may think they talk feelingly, they may relish their talk, may imagine they perceive a divine savour in it, as David did in Achitophele, . . . and yet all may prove nothing.

156. The book of Scripture is the interpreter of the book of nature two ways, viz., by declaring to us those spiritual mysteries that are indeed signified and typified in the constitution of the natural world; and secondly, in actually making application of the signs and types in the book of nature as representations of those spiritual mysteries in many instances.

157. The earth or this earthly world does by men's persons as it does by their bodies: it devours men and eats them up. As we see this our mother that brought us forth and at whose breasts we are nourished is cruel to us, she is hungry for the flesh of her children, and swallows up mankind, one generation after another, in the grave, and is insatiable in her appetite. So she does mystically those that live by the breasts of the earth and depend on worldly things for happiness; the earth undoes and ruins them. It makes them miserable forever, it devours and eats up the inhabitants thereof according to the evil report that the spies brought up of the land of Canaan. (Num. 13.32)

158. The way in which most of the things we use are serviceable to us and answer their end is in their being strained, or hard pressed, or violently agitated. Thus the way in which the bow answers its end is in hard straining of it to shoot the arrow and do the execution; the bow that won't bear straining is good for nothing. So it is with a staff that a man walks with: it answers its end in being hard pressed. So it is with many of the members of our bodies, our teeth, our feet, etc. And so with most of the utensils of life, an ox, a saw, a flail, a rope, a chain, etc. They are usefull and answer their end by some violent straining, pressure, agitation, collision, or impulsion. And they that are so weak as not to bear the trial of such usage are good for nothing. Here is a lively representation of the way in which true and sincere saints (which

are often in Scripture represented as God's instruments or utensils) answer God's end, and serve and glorify Him in it by enduring temptation, going through hard labour, suffering, or self-denial, or such service as strains hard upon nature and self. Hypocrites are like a broken tooth, a foot out of joint, a broken staff, a deceitfull bow which fails when pressed or strained.

159. The higher anything is raised up in the air, the more swift and violent is its fall. The higher the place is that any one falls from, the more fatal is his fall. And the higher any body falls from, if it falls into water, the more violently and deeply is it plunged. Thus it is in religion. Thus it is with backsliders and hypocrites, and them that are rested high in knowledge, wealth, and worldly dignity, and also in spiritual priviledge and in profession and religious illuminations and comforts.

160. As spiders when shut up together so that they can't catch flies devour one another, so the devils, after the day of judgment when they shall be shut in their consummate misery and can devour the miserable children of men no more, will be each other's tormenters.

161. Water in artificial water-works rises no higher than the spring from whence it comes unless by a superadded strength from some other cause. So nothing in men can rise higher than the principle from whence it comes. Nature can't be improved by men themselves so as to bring them to any qualification higher than natural principles, more excellent in their kind than self-love, etc.

162. True grace is like true gold: it will bear the trial of the furnace without diminishing. And it is like the true diamond: it will bear a smart stroke of the hammer and will not break.

163. The oar in which the gold and silver naturally [are mixed] till refined by fire, the stone in which the gem naturally is bedded till separated by hard blows, the husk and chaff in which the good

grain is till separated by threshing and winnowing, the shell and
pod in which the kernell is till beaten off, are all representation[s]
of the mixtures that attend grace in the hearts of saints in this
world, which are separated more and more by affliction, as by a
furnace or threshing, etc. (to which it is compared in Scripture),
and finally by the pains of death. This mixture is called dross
and tin.

164. For texts confirming observations that may be made, see
innumerable places of Scripture representing spiritual things by
things appertaining to husbandry, fields, vineyards, trees, corn,
fruit, etc. See texts in Mr. Flavel's *Husbandry Spiritualized*.

165. The seed that is sown in the ground, from the very time
that it is sown till it be fully ripe, is ever exposed to one thing or
other that tends to annoy and destroy it. When it is first sown, it
is liable to be picked up by the fowls. When it first puts forth, it is
liable to be soon eaten by worms, either above or under ground, or
to be scorched by the summer sun, and if it bears this, it is liable to
be choked with weeds or thorns. And when it is grown tall and the
fruit put forth but yet green, it is liable to be greatly injured by
honey-dews. So it is with seeming grace, and in some respects
with real grace in the soul. There are various kinds of apostates
and hypocrites; some are overcome and overthrown by one trial,
others by another. Some hold out for a shorter and others for a
longer time; some bear trials that others are overset by, and yet
at last comes a trial that overthrows them. But of all trials, great
worldly prosperity and great seeming spiritual prosperity and
honour is the greatest. This, like a honey-dew, may kill those that
have born other trials. So true grace is assaulted and annoyed in
all its different stages with various enemies. And even when the
saints are arrived at a great height in religion and are tall Christians, and near to God, and their fruit put forth but not yet become
solid and ripe, are greatly in danger by a honey-dew, i.e., their
great spiritual prosperity and sweet joys and comfort bring them
into a languishing, sorrowfull state through spiritual pride.

166. There are two quite different things intended by the God of nature and disposer of all things to be signified by the GRAFTING of trees. And therefore some things in grafting by no means agree with one of these things, and other things that by no means agree with the other. 1. The first thing signified is the ingrafting the soul into Christ: in this Christ is the stock and the believer is the cyon or branch, who is cut out of its natural stock, taken out of the stock of the first Adam wherein he grew by nature, for a corrupt nature is mortified. He is cut off from his own stock and root, emptied of himself, brought to self-denial and renunciation of his own righteousness and dignity, and is weaned from this world, is cut off from the stock by which it naturally grew in the earth, and this as it were by a keen knife, by the cutting work of the law and of repentance, and is brought to Christ as a scion is to a new stock and root, and united so to him as to have a vital union with him and become a member or branch in him, and has a new head of vital influence, derives vital influence from Christ, and lives by his life, and flourishes and increases and looks forth and brings forth fruit by virtue of union with him. In these things the change made in the state of a soul at conversion is livelily represented by the ingrafting of trees. But then there are some things in the grafting of trees that by no means agrees to this, viz., the stock conforms to the scyion and not the scyon to the stock. The top of the stock is changed and meliorated by the scyion, and not the scyion by the stock. The scyion is taken out of a good tree that bears good fruit and grafted into a bad tree that is wild by nature, that is barren or bears barren and useless fruit, and it is the stock that is changed for the better and not the scyon. The good fruit that the grafted tree bears is the scyon's fruit and not the fruit of the stock and root. And therefore this is not all that is intended to be signified by ingrafting, but,

2. There is another great thing intended that God aimed at no less, which those latter things agree to wherein Christ is not the stock but the branch, as here (after the branch or the tender twig, as the word in the original signifies): He is the man whose name

is the BRANCH, and the thing signified is the union of Christ the heavenly branch with mankind, and particularly:

(1) Christ's incarnation, whereby this divine person, this branch of paradise, was taken, as it were, from heaven its natural soil, taken out of the bosom of his Father from whom he eternally proceeded or sprang, and was, as it were, cut off from Him, from the glory he had with Him before the world was, and emptied himself, in his humiliation to be ingrafted into the mean, inferiour race of mankind, that may, soly by reason of the manner of its propagation, fitly be compared to a tree with many branches from one seed or root, and is often compared to a tree in Scripture. (See Misc. No. 991.) Christ was, as it were, cut off from his natural stock in his humiliation; he emptied himself, he was in some sense cut off from the glory that he had with the Father before the world was during his humbled state. And he took the human nature that was comparatively a mean, worthless, barren stock. This human nature was not changed by Christ's taking it upon him, though it be dignified and its fruit exceedingly changed; even as the stock is not changed by the scyon's being grafted upon it, it remains human nature still, and will forever. Christ is true man still as well as God, and so will remain to all eternity, but this nature is infinitely dignified and its fruit infinitely changed for the better, by virtue of the scion that is implanted into it. The nature of neither stock nor scyion is changed, but both remain the same they were before, though both are united into one tree and live by one life, so neither the human nature [nor the divine] are changed one into the other, though both are united in one person.

(2) Another thing intended is Christ's being ingrafted into the church of Christ, which was by his uniting himself with believers in his incarnation, whereby he became a member of the church, a branch of the church, a son of this mother and a brother of believers, agreeable to the church's wish, Cant. 8.1: O that thou were as my brother that sucked the breasts of my mother. The church of Christ is often represented by a tree in Scripture. The tree was planted in Abraham; every member of the church

is a branch of that tree, and Christ is the seed of Abraham. He is the great *seed* of Abraham, to whom and in whom the promise was made, Gal. 3.19, 16, and it is by this seed or this BRANCH that the blessing is to the tree. All the fruit of the tree is by the ingrafting this tender twig into it. This ingrafted branch bears all. The tree in itself bears no good fruit, it is very sowr, but this ingrafted branch furnishes it. This fruit or ability to bear fruit is everlasting; there is fruit to God and his glory, and that we receive ourselves in a harvest of joy and comfort and in everlasting life. The stock remains the same, but the fruit is altered. So, by Christ being ingrafted, the faculties of the soul are the same; there is the same human nature still, but there is new fruit of grace, holy exercises and practice, and true blessedness. The stock is the same, but the sap, by the union to the cyon, is changed and made better; so the soul, by a vital union with Christ and by the faculties' being as it were swallowed up in Christ, are altered, sanctified, and sweetened. It is observable that a good scyon flourishes best in a sowr stock; so Christ has more glory in saving the sinfull and miserable, for the sick need a phisician, and Christ came not to call the righteous but sinners to repentance.

3. Christ by his incarnation and union with men was ingrafted into David's royal stock. He is often represented as the branch of his family whence it should have all its glory and bear all its fruit. It is by this branch that the royal family of Israel feeds all the world with its fruit, as was said in some sense of Nebuchadnezzer under the type of a great tree. This is that tender twig of the royal family of David spoken of.

This blessed branch in the stock of Abraham and David, though it grows on the stock and flourishes from the root, yet proceeds not thence in the way of natural propagation as the natural branches do, but is ingrafted in.

4. Christ is ingrafted into every believer; every believer is ingrafted into Christ, and Christ is ingrafted into every believer. For the believer is not only in Christ, but Christ in him. Christ is born in the soul of the believer and brought forth there, and every believer is a mother of Christ. Grace in the soul is the infant Christ

there, a tender twig ingrafted from an heavenly stock in the soul by which it bears all its fruit. The nature is sanctified, the sap sweetened, and the tree made fruitfull. Christ is ingrafted by the word's being ingrafted, which is able to save the soul. Not only the written or spoken word is ingrafted but the personal word, which eminently is able to save the soul. Grace in the soul is Christ there. This is represented as a seed implanted there, and may as fitly be represented as a twig or bud ingrafted there, which sprouts and flourishes and brings forth fruit. In order to this ingrafting, both must be cut off the stock and the branch: the stock must be cut off its natural products; branches and fruit of its own righteousness must be cut off, that Christ may be ingrafted in the room of them, and the fruit of worldly enjoyments and carnal happiness must be cut off. And Christ the cyon is cut off from his natural stock in his humiliation, to make way for his being vitally united to the vile and miserable sinner. The change made in the stock when the scyon is ingrafted into it fitly represents the change made in man by regeneration. Something is destroyed, and that which is new put into the room of it, and something remains. The old branches and fruit are all cut off and perish, new branches and fruit entirely new succeed: this fitly represents the change of dispositions, affections, and practices. But the old stock and root remains: this fitly represents the same faculties' remaining, the same human nature, that is, as it were, the substance or substratum of these properties, both old and new, and on which both old and new fruits do grow.

Upon the whole, it is to be noted that when a tree that is bad by nature is grafted or has a good cyon inserted into it, all the old branches are cut off and do perish, this not at once if the tree is grown to any bigness and has many branches when the ingrafting is done, but as the ingrafted branch grows and flourishes, so the husbandman gradually cuts away the other branches to make room for it, till at length none are left but the ingrafted branch, and all the sap of the tree runs into that, and the tree becomes wholly a new tree. So it is Christ the heavenly branch is ingrafted into the bad tree of the race of mankind, and all other branches perish but only this ingrafted branch and the branches that grow from it. All perish in hell, and by degrees there is a visible destruction of them in this world, till at length only this cyon and the branches that grow from it shall remain, and all things shall be made new. There was, soon after this cyon was ingrafted, a great destruction of the nation of the unbelieving Jews, and after that a great destruction of the heathen in the Roman Empire in Constantine's time, when the branch was grown much bigger. And hereafter will there be a yet vastly greater destruction of the wicked all over the world, and the earth shall be every where in a great measure emptied of wicked men, and this ingrafted branch shall spread and fill the earth. And after this, at the end, every branch and twig that don't proceed from this cyon shall be perfectly destroyed and the whole tree shall be made [new]. God shall say, Behold, I make all things new, and there shall be a new heaven and a new earth.

And so it shall be in the tree of Abraham, the visible Church of God. Christ was the cyon that was ingrafted into this tree, and the other branches must all be cut off, but only they which grow from this cyon. At the first insertion of the cyon there was a great cutting off of old branches of this tree in the destruction of the Jews, and there will be a still greater at the destruction of antichrist, and all remains of the old branches shall be cut off at the end of the world. So it was with respect to the tree of the royal family of David when the cyon was ingrafted: many other branch[es] of that family were, as it were, cut off by putting an end to the genealogy or perishing of all records of their families. And in a particular soul, when this heavenly seed is implanted in it or this heavenly twig or bud ingrafted, the old nature is at once mortified and old branches and fruits cut off by conviction and repentance, and the remains of them are more and more cut off and cleared away as the new branch increases, till at length there remains no other branch, and no fruit is brought forth but what grows on this branch, and so the tree is entirely renewed.

This latter signification of ingrafting seems to be chiefly intended by the author of nature, because He thought that great and glorious mystery of Christ's incarnation and union with mankind most worthy to be much showed forth and observed.

"Miscellanies," No. 991: The race of mankind are like a tree, that comes from one seed, but runs out into many millions of branches. Some parts of this tree is holy; there is evermore a holy branch in the tree that belongs to God, which is called the branch of God's planting, Isa. 60.21; though sometimes it be but a little twig. In all its successive productions and multiplicated ramifications, there is an holy line of branches that do in some respect grow one out of another, and commonly in the natural ramification or ordinary generation. Other parts of the tree, that are not actually holy branches (i.e., the parts already put forth [that] are not holy) yet have an holy or elect seed in them, or an holy bud; though in some so deeply enfolded, that it is a great way off from putting forth or unfolding, and there remains a great number of successions of germinations or ramifications before its turn comes to put forth. Those branches that had the holy seed in them have in past ages of the world been but few; all other branches but only those, the great husbandman cuts off from one age to another. Thus in the old world the tree was grown very great, and its branches were innumerable, but all were cut off at once but one, that one twig which alone had any of the holy seeds in it. . . .[18]

And there remains yet a more dreadfull destruction of men than has perhaps ever yet been since the flood, which is spoken of, Rev. 19, at the latter end, just before the setting up of Christ's kingdom through the earth, which will be the greatest and chief pruning of the tree to prepare and make room for the great and principal putting forth of the elect seed, the holy bud that had been preserved in the tree by the special care of providence from the beginning of the world and that had lain hid in the branches of the tree through all ages, being reserved for this appointed time for their germination. And then the tree shall be abundantly watered by the showers of heaven and the holy seed shall flourish as the grass of the earth. They shall spring up as among the grass and as willows by the watercourses. The tree shall blossom abundantly and the fruit of it shall shine like Lebanon. God will be as the dew unto Israel, and he shall grow as the lily and cast forth his roots as Lebanon, his branches shall spread, and his beauty shall be as the olive tree and his smell as Lebanon.

Thus we see how God from age to age lops off other branches that put forth from the tree beside the elect line, and that have not in them the holy seed to be the substance and preservation of them, and only those branches are left wherein is this holy seed. And it is this holy seed, which is God's part, the first fruits to God and the Lamb, that upholds the world, and keeps it in being. When once all this fruit is brought forth, and ripened, the world will come to an end.

In this tree there is one branch that is called by way of eminency, in Scripture, THE BRANCH. This is eminently the holy seed or bud that lay hid in the tree for four thousand years, and was upheld in a certain line or succession of branches before it put forth; it is called THE BRANCH because it was infinitely of the greatest value in the sight of God, and it was that branch that naturally comprehended all the rest; all are engrafted into it, whereby they have life and holiness; all are united by a divine union to it, and are holy branches no otherwise than as branches growing out of this branch, or as parts and members of it. God, through all that four thousand years before this branch put forth, took great and extraordinary care of that part of the tree in which it lay hid. He once destroyed the whole when it became a great tree that filled the world with branches, but only one twig that had His holy seed in it; and then the tree sprouted again, and many branches grew out of it. He separated that twig that had this eminent seed in it in the call of Abraham, and took great and distinguishing care of that nation that was the branch of mankind that contained the holy seed. This was the vine God brought out of Egypt, and cast out the heathen before it, and planted it, and the branch which God made strong for Himself, . . . from age to age wonderfully distinguishing it from all other nations. And since this branch has sprouted and has been cut off, God has taken it, and planted it in the mountain of the height of Israel, and caused it to flourish and bring forth numerous branches, and overspread [a] great part of the world, and will cause its branches to fill the whole world, and will lop off all other branches.

God commonly prunes the tree very much by lopping off many branches just before any remarkable putting forth and flourishing of the holy seed in a great number of buds and branches, to make room for these holy branches, to purge the tree, and the better to fit it to bear much fruit. Hence commonly those who are the subjects of remarkably great spiritual mercies, a distinguished shower of divine blessing, are a remnant after a great destruction, the remnant of the tree after a great cutting off and casting away of reprobate branches. . . .

So when a people or a family is destroyed without remnant, it is in Scripture compared to utterly destroying a tree or a plant, root and branches. . . . Because the holy seed that is in a nation is its greatest preservative, and that which affectually secures it and all the world from utter destruction, therefore the future flourishing of this holy seed in a nation, and especially the future birth of Christ, who is by way of eminency THE BRANCH, is mentioned as a sign of preservation of a nation in great danger. . . .

167. The manner of taking and destroying almost all kinds of wild beasts and birds in traps, pits, snares, and nets, by bait, laying before the creature that is to be taken and destroyed what is agreeable to its appetite, is a lively representation of what comes to pass in the moral and spiritual world.

168. There are most representations of divine things in things that are most in view or that we are chiefly concerned in: as in the sun, his light and other influences and benefits; in the other heavenly bodies; in our own bodies; in our state, our families and commonwealths; and in this business that mankind do principally follow, viz., husbandry.

169. IMAGES of divine things: There are some types of divine things, both in Scripture and also in the works of nature and constitution of the world, that are much more lively than others, everything seems to arise that way; and in some things the image is very lively, in others less lively, in others the image but faint and the resemblance in but few particulars, with many things wherein there is a dissimilitude. God has ordered things in this respect much as He has in the natural world. He hath made man the head and end of this lower creation, and there are innumerable creatures that have some image of what is in men, but in an infinite

variety of degrees. Animals have much more of a resemblance of what is in men than plants, plants much more than things inanimate. Some of the animals have a very great resemblance of what is in men, some in some respects, and others in others, and some have much less. Some are so little above plants that there is some difficulty in determining whether they be plants or animals. And even among plants, there are numberless in some things there seems to be, as it were, only some feeble attempts of nature towards a vegetable life, and it is difficult to know what order of being they belong to. There is a like difference and variety in the light held forth by types as there is in the light of the stars in the night. Some are very bright, some you can scarcely determine whether there be a star there or no, and the like different degrees, as there is the light of twighlight, signifying the approaching sun.

170. It is in the natural world as it is in the spiritual world in this respect: that there are many imitations and false resemblances of most things that are the more excellent in the natural world. Thus there are many stones that have a resemblance of diamonds that are not true diamonds. There are many ways of counterfeiting gold. The balm of Gilead and many others of the most excellent medicines are many ways sophisticated. So is grace counterfeited.

171. Concerning the blossoming and ripening of fruits and other things of that nature: The first puttings forth of the tree in order to fruit make a great show and are pleasant to the eye, but the fruit then is very small and tender. Afterwards, when there is less show, the fruit is increased. So it often is at first conversion. There are flowing affections, passionate joys, that are the flower that soon falls off, etc. The fruit when young is very tender, easily hurt with frost or heat or vermin or any thing that touches it. So it is with young converts, Cant. 2.15: Take us the foxes, the little foxes, that spoil the vines, for our vines have tender grapes.

Fruit on the tree or in the field is not in its fixed and ultimate state, the state where it properly answers its end, but in a state wholly subordinate and preparatory to another. So it is with the saints. The fruit while it stands in the field or hangs on the tree till fully ripe and the time of gathering comes, is in a progressive state, growing in perfection. So it is with grace in the saints. Many kinds of fruit have a great deal of bitterness and sourness while green, and much that is crude and unwholesome, which, as it ripens, becomes sweeter, the juices purer, the crude parts are removed. The burning heat of the summer sun purges away that which is crude, sour, and unwholesome, and refines the fruit and ripens it and fits it more for use, which burning heat withers and destroys those fruits that have not substance in them. So young converts have a remaining sourness and bitterness. They have a great mixture in their experiences and religious exercises, but as they ripen for heaven, they are more purified. Their experiences become purer, their tempers are more mollified and sweetened with meekness and Christian love, and this by afflictions, persecutions, and occasions of great self-denial, or in one word by the cross of Christ, whereas those trials bring hypocrites to nothing.

Green fruit hangs fast to the tree, but when it is ripe, it is loose and easily picked. Wheat, while it is green in the field, sucks and draws for nourishment from the ground, but when it is ripe, it draws no more. So a saint when ripe for heaven is weaned from the world.

172. Husbandmen are wont to PRUNE their trees after the dead time of winter, a little before the spring, when the time approaches for them to put forth and blossom with new life and rejoicing. So God is wont to wound His saints a little before He revives them after falls and long seasons of deadness, and to purge them and prepare them for revival and benefit. So He is wont to wound and purge His church, and to lead them into sorrows; He will bring them out the wilderness and speak comfortably to them.

173. Tears flowing from the eyes in sorrow typifies the godly sorrow flowing from spiritual sight or knowledge.

174. Observe the danger of being led by fancy: as he that looks on the fire or on the clouds, giving way to his fancy, easily imagines he sees images of men or beasts in those confused appearances.

175. There is nothing here below that reaches heaven, no, not the highest things, but all fall immensely short of it. Many things, before we experience [them], seem to reach heaven: the tops of high mountains seem to touch the sky, and when we are in the plain and look up to their tops, it seems to us as though, if we were there, we could touch the sun, moon, and stars. But when we are come, we seem as far off from those heavenly things as ever. So there is nothing here below by which we can attain to happiness, though there be many of the high and great things of the world that seem to others that don't enjoy them as though happiness was to be reached by them; yet those that have experience find happiness as far from them as from those that are in a lower state of life.

176. A HOG is in many respects an image of an earthly, carnal man, and among others in this: that he is good for nothing till death, not good to bear or carry as the horse, nor to draw as the ox, or to give milk as the cow, nor to cloath as the sheep, but is fed only for the slaughter.

177. It is observed of the CROCODILE that it cometh of an egg no bigger than a goose egg, yet grows till he is fifteen cubits long (Pliny says thirty). He is also long-lived and grows as long as he lives (See Spencer's *Similies and Sentences*, p. 68.[19]) And how terrible a creature does he become, how destructive and hard to be destroyed. So sin is comparatively easily crushed in the egg, taken in its beginning; but if let alone, what head does it get, how great and strong, terrible and destructive does it become, and hard to kill, and grows as long as it lives. So it is with sin or Satan's interest in particular persons. So it is with his interest in towns, countreys, and empires and the world of mankind. How small was Satan's interest in the old world, beginning in Cain's family, but what did it come to before the flood? How small was idolatry in its be-

ginnings after the flood, but how did it carry the world before it afterwards, and hold it for many ages, growing stronger and greater and worse and worse? So it was with the kingdom of antichrist, and so it was with Satan's Mahometan kingdom, and so it will probably be with the last apostacy before the end of time.

178. "The wheels of a WATCH or a CLOCK move contrary one to another, some one way, some another, yet all serve the intent of the workman to shew the time, or to make the clock to strike. So in the world the providence of God may seem to run cross to his promises: one man takes this way, another takes that way; good men go one way, wicked men another; yet all in the conclusion accomplish the will, and center in the purpose of God the great creator of all things." (Spencer's *Similies and Sentences*, p. 69.)

179. The MOLE opens not his eyes till he be dead. (See Spencer's *Similies and Sentences*, p. 69, n. 288.)

180. The day of JUDGMENT and the great things that will then be to be seen is in some respect or other represented by most of those occasions in which mankind are wont to gather together in great assemblies and to make a publick, solemn, or joyfull appearance. The great assemblies and processions that are wont to [occur] at the coronation of princes are a shadow of the great assembly and glorious procession that will be at the end of the world, when the saints shall receive their crown of glory with Christ, as well as the ascension when he was crowned in his person. The great assemblies that sometimes are at courts of judicature on some great trial and the mighty assemblies that are at executions also are a little shadow of what will be at that time. The joyfull assembly, the splendid show, and the solemn processions that oftentimes are at weddings do shadow forth what will be then. The solemn, magnificent, and joyfull assemblies, equipage, and processions on great triumphs do also represent what will be then.

181. Serpents gradually swallow many of those animals that are their prey; they are too big for them to swallow at once, but they draw them down by little and little, till they are wholly swallowed and are past recovery. This represents the way in which Satan destroys multitudes of men that have had so good an education or so much conviction and light and common grace that they are too big to be swallowed at once. It also livelily represents his way of corrupting and prevailing against Christian countreys and churches, and against even some of the saints with respect to some particular errours and corruptions that he draws them into for a season.

182. When summer has continued uninterrupted for some time, then begin to come many flies and other insects that are hurtful and noisom. But after they are come, they remain long after the weather grows cool, and it must be a very hard frost to kill [them]. A small frost may chill them and restrain them, but they will revive again at the return of every warm day. So a long continuance of a summer of prosperity, of outward or spiritual comforts, breeds hurtful and noisom and corrupting insects, as it were, in the soul. Many evil things contrary to the humility and simplicity that is in Christ gradually creep in till they swarm. So it is in a particular person, and so it is in the church of God, and after they have got in and have got foot hold, it is a hard thing to root them out. If the prosperity and comforts are withdrawn, there must be very much of the contrary before they will be killed. These insects in summer signify the same with the worms in the manna.

183. The spiritual restoration of the world is compared to the renewing of the face of the earth in the SPRING in Ps. 147.18 (with the context).

184. That dominion of the stars in the earth spoken of Job 38. 31–33, is an image of the dominion of angels in the earth.

185. That the sun is designed by God as a type of Christ may be argued from Scripture, not only by Christ's being frequently represented by it, being called the sun of righteousness, the light of the world, etc., but also by the sun's withdrawing its light when Christ was crucified,—as it were conforming to its antitype, as the veil of the temple did at the same time that [was] rent when Christ's flesh (which by the Apostle's testimony is its antitype) was rent or his animal nature destroyed. And at the same time, the light of the sun was extinguished when the life of Christ, its antitype, was extinguished. Christ rising with the sun at his resurrection is another argument of the same thing.

186. When the sun withdraws, beasts of prey go forth to destroy, and that is the time for caterpillars and noisom insects and hurtful vermine in general to go forth to prey upon the trees and plants. But when the sun rises, they retire, well representing the nature of evil spirits and the corruptions of the heart, and wicked men and the enemies of our souls, and the church of God in general.

187. BREAD: It seems to be because that those things which grain, as it were, suffers before it is fit for our food, and particularly threshing, represents the sufferings of Christ, that God ordered that the altar of Israel should be built by David on a threshing floor, which was the place where the temple was built and all the sacrifices of Israel thenceforward were offered. And therefore also the same instruments that were used in threshing [were used] in burning the sacrifice, because in both they typified the instruments of Christ's sufferings. And the oxen, who by their labours trod out the corn, were offered on the altar, because they represented Christ, who was not only the sacrifice but the priest, too, was active in his own sufferings, and so provided us heavenly bread. Hence also Gideon was ordered to build an altar to God at or by the place where he threshed wheat, and also near the wine press, Judg. 6.11, 19–21, 26. The manner of

procuring wine in a wine-press, representing the shedding the blood as the threshing wheat for our bread, signifies the sufferings inflicted on his body. (See Image 197.)

188. As all the good and happiness of mankind comes by redemption and salvation, all his light arises out of darkness, all his happiness out of misery, all his wealth out of the most extreme poverty and his life out of death, agreeable to those circumstances of mankind and the great design and methods of God's grace towards him through the saviour, it is ordered that so many of our outward mercies and good things are given in a way of deliverance, protection, or remedy from some calamity we have been the subjects of or are exposed to. Thus God rather gives us clothing to cover our nakedness than to make us without any deformity and nakedness we should be ashamed of. He rather gives us food to preserve us from famishing and wasting away and perishing miserably, to which we are continually exposed, and to satisfy our hunger, rather than to make our bodies such as should not be exposed to waste and consume and need continuall repairs or [to] make [them] without hunger. So God gives us drink to satisfy our thirst rather than to make us without thirst. He gives us means to defend us from cold and heat and showers and the inclemencies of the weather [rather] than to make the atmosphere to be alwaies serene and temperate. He gives us breath constantly to refresh and give new life to our vitals and blood, and [to] preserve [us] from death that otherwise we should be exposed to every moment, rather than to make our bodies with a permanent life and so that our vital and animal forces should not need continued refreshment and revival. He gives us sleep to relieve us, and gives us comfortable rest when weary, rather than that we should not be liable to weariness. He gives us moons to enlighten us in the night, as by the light of a candle, etc., rather than that we should have no darkness, or no more than during the necessary time of sleep. He gives means of defence from wild beasts, from noisom vermine and insects, rather than there should

be no such noxious things that we should be exposed to. He has provided many things of medicinal and sanative nature as a remedy in case of wounds and sickness rather than that we should be liable to none of these maladies. But here it is observable that though these mercies are thus given as a protection or remedy from evils and calamities we are subject to or exposed [to], yet they are many of them something beyond a meer remedy. Thus we have food not only to keep us from famishing and remove the pain of hunger, but to entertain and delight us; so we have not only clothes to cover our nakedness, but to adorn us, and so of other things. As God in the redemption of Christ does not only provide for our salvation from misery, but provides for us positive blessedness and glory.

189. (Vid. Images 68 and 48.) The seeming suffering of our food by being boiled, roasted, etc., to cleanse it from its crudities and impurities, to fit it to be wholesome, pleasant food for us, also represents God's dealings with His people, with particular persons and elect nations, and His visible church, to fit it to be, as it were, food for Him. (See Jer. 2.13.)

190. In the conception of an animal and formation of the embrio, the first thing appearing is the punctum saliens or the heart, which beats as soon as it exists. And from thence the other parts gradually appear, as though they all gradually proceeded and branched forth from that beating point. This is a lively image of the manner of the formation of the new creature. The first thing is a new heart, a new sense and inclination that is a principle of new life, a principle that, however small, is active and has vigour and power, and, as it more beats and struggles, thirsts after holiness, aims at and tends to every thing that belongs to the new creature, and has within it the foundation and source of the whole. It aims at perfection, and from thence are the issues of life. From thence the various things that belong to the new creature all proceed and branch forth and gradually appear, and that more and more. And this principle, from its first ex-

istence, never ceases to exert itself, until the new creature be compleat and comes to its proper perfection.

191. A bubble that is blown up, when it is come to be largest of all and full of fine colours, is near breaking, which is a lively image of earthly glory, which very commonly, when it is come to the height, is near its end and commonly goes out and vanishes away in a moment, and a proper type of the men of this world, who place their happiness in the things of this life, who, when they are most swollen with worldly prosperity and are in the midst of their honours, wealth and pleasures, and glory most in these things, do commonly die. Death dashes all their glory to pieces in a moment, Ps. 37.35, 36: I have seen the wicked in great power and spreading himself like a green bay tree, yet he passed away, and lo, he was not, yea, I sought him, but he could not be found. And many places in Job; Hos. 10.7: As for Samaria, her king is cut off as the foam upon the water.

192. When the fruit is ripe, it is easily gathered; it does not cleave fast to the tree, but is ready to quit it, and is picked without rending or making any wound. So is a saint that is ripe for heaven, he easily quits this world. (Job 5.26.)

193. The head supplies, animates, and directs the body, but the body supports and bears the weight of the head. This is an image of what should be between civil and ecclesiastical heads of societies and their people.

194. Many hypocrites are like wood that lies above ground and has no root at all in the ground, that yet will grow in the spring and put forth boughs like a living plant; but this growth is short-lived, it will not endure the trial of the burning heat of midsummer. (See Matt. 13.6.)

195. We can't go about the world but our feet will grow dirty. So in whatever sort of worldly business men do with their hands,

their hands will grow dirty and will need washing from time to time, which is to represent the fulness of this world of pollution. It is full of sin and temptations. In all their goings they are imperfect and polluted with sin, every step they take is attended with sin. So all the works that they do are polluted. They can perform no service, no business, but they contract their guilt and defilement, that they need the renewed washing of the blood of Christ.

196. The meat and drink of mankind comes down from heaven in the rain, and even our clothing and habitations, and even the substance of our bodies, and is mostly of the very substance of the rain, which very naturally leads us to the fountain of all our mercies, and teaches us that we are fed and maintained by those things that are wholly the fruits of God's bounty and are universally and entirely dependent on Him.

197. (See Image 187.) It is evident the baking of bread is a type of the sufferings of Christ, because the shew bread is said to be an offering made by fire unto the Lord (Lev. 24.7, 9), but it was an offering made by fire no otherwise than it was baked with fire. But all the offerings made by fire, by the Mosaic law, were types of Christ undoubtedly, and their suffering the fire was also undoubtedly a type of Christ's suffering.

198. As the silk-worm, so the bee seems to be designed as a type of Christ, who having spent his life in gathering, with the greatest labour and industry, and laying up in store the most delicious food, having completed his work is killed, and by his death yields all his stores for the refreshment and delight of his murderers. (See Hervey, *Meditations*, I, 269, 270.) [20]

199. See blank Bible, p. 656, col. 1 at the top of the col.

"Notes on the Scriptures," at beginning of New Testament: It is evident by John 11.50–52 that occurrences in the history of the New

Testament as well as Old have a mystery in them, and that they are ordered on purpose to represent and shadow forth spiritual things.

200. Those machines for the measuring of time are by wheels and wheels within wheels, some lesser, some greater, some of quicker, others of slower revolution, some moving one way, others another, some wheels dependent on others, and all connected together, all adjusted one to another, and all conspiring to bring about the same effect, lively represents the course of things in time from day to day, from year to year, and from age to age, as ordered and gouverned by divine providence.

201. It is observed by the prophet Jeremiah (Chap. 32.8) concerning only a common providential occurrence that it was the word of the Lord, that is, that it [was] designedly ordered to be a special signification of God's mind and will as much as His word. By which it appears that God don't think this a thing improper or unbecoming of His wisdom, thus designedly to contrive His works and to dispose things in the common affairs of the world in such a manner as [to] represent diverse things and signify His mind as truly as His word.

202. If even the most GLORIOUS HEAVENLY BODIES are viewed narrowly, as when we view them with glasses, they appear with SPOTS, even that most bright and glorious of all visible things, the SUN, which denotes the imperfection of the most excellent of created beings, Job 25.5: Behold even to the moon and it shineth not, yea, the stars are not pure in His sight.

203. EXTERNAL THINGS are intended to be IMAGES of things spiritual, moral, and divine. The following words are taken from Turnbull's *Moral Philosophy*, pp. 54, 55:
"Now it has been often observed that such is the analogy between sensible and moral objects that there is none of the latter sort that may not be clothed with a sensible form or image and represented to us as it were in a material shape and hue. So

true is [this] that not only are wit and poetry owned to take place only in consequence of this analogy or resemblance of moral and natural ideas, but even all language is confessed to be originally taken from sensible objects or their properties and effects—words cannot express any moral objects but by exciting pictures of them in our minds; but all words being originally expressive of sensible qualities, no words can express moral ideas but so far as there is such an analogy betwixt the natural and moral world that objects in the latter may be shadowed forth, pictured, or imaged to us by some resemblances to them in the former— and so far as language can go in communicating sentiments, so far we have an indisputable proof of analogy between the sensible and the moral world; and consequently of wonderful wisdom and goodness in adjusting sensible and moral relations and connexions one to another: the sensible world to our minds and reciprocally the connexions of things, relative to our moral powers, to the connection of things that constitute the sensible world. It is this analogy that makes the beauty, propriety, and force of words expressive of moral ideas by conveying pictures of them into the mind.

"All the phrases among the antients used to signify the beauty, harmony, and consistency of virtuous manners are taken from the beauty of sensible forms in nature or in the arts which imitate nature, musick, painting, etc.—so that here we have a clear proof of that analogy between the moral world or moral effects and the natural world or sensible effects without which language could not be a moral paintress or paint moral sentiments and affections and their effects." *Ibid.*, pp. 145, 146.

And the same author, in his second volume entitled *Christian Philosophy*, pp. 178, 179, says: "There is a much more exact correspondence and analogy between the natural and moral world than superficial observers are apt to imagine or take notice of." Again, *ibid.*, pp. 180, 181: "No one can be acquainted with nature or indeed with the imitative arts, with poetry in particular, without perceiving and admiring the correspondence between the sensible and moral world from which arises such a beautiful, rich source of imagery in poetry, and without which there could be no such thing." [21]

204. There is a sort of OWLS that make a screaming, shrieking, dolorous noise; these are birds of the night that shun daylight and live in darkness. And those creatures, that are in Scripture called DRAGONS, it seems used to make a doleful, screaming, wailing noise. Both which are referred to in Mic. 1.8: I will make a wailing like dragons and mourning as the owls; Job 30. 28, 29: I went mourning without the sun, I stood up, and I cried in the congregation, I am a brother to dragons and a companion to owls. The wailing of these dragons and owls represents the misery and wailing of devils, who are often called dragons, and of other spirits that dwell in eternal darkness.

205. The time for WEEDING a GARDEN is when it has newly rained upon it. Otherwise, if you go to pull up the weeds, you will pull up the good herbs and plants with them. So the time for purging the church of God is a time of revival of religion. It can't be so well done at another time. The state of the church of God will not so well bear it. It will neither so well bear the searching, trying doctrines of religion in their close application, nor a thorough ecclesiastical administration and discipline. Nor will it bear at another time to be purged from its old corruptions, customs, ceremonies, etc.

206. IMAGES of divine things in God's works: "It is certain, that the word hieroglyphicks which the Greeks made use of to design those symbolical characters (used by the antients) signifies a sacred graving or sculpture, because that way of writing was first consecrated to preserve and transmit to posterity some idea of the mysteries of religion. The first sages of the most remote antiquity made use of sensible signs to represent intellectual and spiritual truths. All the different parts of nature are employed in this sacred language."—"The source of this primitive hieroglyphical language seems to have been the persuasion

of the great truth that the visible world is representative of the
invisible, that the properties, forms, and motions of the one
were copies, images, and shadows of the attributes, qualities, and
laws of the other." Ramsay, *Principles*, II, 11, 12.[22]

207. "Creaturae illae rationales simul sumtae vocantur mundus
spiritualis, opposite ad mundum aspectabilem sive corporeum,
etiam Respublica Spirituum et Civitas Dei.

"Hic Fundamenta Theologiae Emblematicae ostendere
possemus, indicando nempe, non minimam sapientiae divinae
partem esse, quod tam admirabilem Harmoniam atque Con-
formitatem inter mundum illum aspectabilem et alterum illum,
qui Mundus spiritualis est, instituerit, ut ea, quae in uno fiunt,
etiam in altero, modo licet differente, fiant; Et uti mundus ille
visibilis Existentiae et attributorum divinorum speculum est,
ita non munus illarum Rerum, quae in Mundo spirituali eveniunt,
speculum esse: Ex sapienti hac atque admirabili omnium divinorum operam Harmonia atque Conformitate nullo deinde
negotio totam illam de Emblematibus Doctrinam deducere nobis liceret. Neque etiam instituti nostri Ratio nobis permittit,
ut multa hic de Praestantia Civitatis illius Dei, sive Respublicae
spirituum peroremus; non tamen a me impetrare possum, quin,
brevissima licet, sed elegantissima Illust. Leibnitii verba de hac
re adducam quae extant in *caussa dei adserta per Justitiam ejus*
'Ipsum autem Bados in divinae sapientia Thesauris, vel in Deo
abscondito, et in universali Rerum Harmonia latet Thesaurum
Mundi Corporei magis magisque ipso Naturae Lumine in hac
vita elegantiam suam nobis ostendit, dum Systemata Macrocosmi
et Microcosmi recentiorum inventis aperiri coepere. Sed pars
Rerum praestantissima, Civitas dei spectaculum est, cujus ad
Pulcritudinem noscendam aliquando demum illustrati divinae
Gloriae Lumine propius admittemur, etc.' " Stapferus, *Theologia
Polem.*, I, 181, 182.[23]

208. Our BREATH to support life, a representation of our dependence on the spirit of God for spiritual life: Cudworth,

Intellec. Syst., p. 428, mentions this, saying of M. Antoninus: "That as our bodies breethe the common air, so should our souls suck and draw in vital breath from the great mind that comprehends the universe, becoming as it were one spirit with the same."

209. The sun a type of Christ: Cudworth's *Intellec. Syst.*, p. 25: "The writer de Placites Philosophorum observes *that Empedocles made two suns: the one archetypal and intelligible, the other apparent or sensible.*"

210. Cudworth's *Intellec. Syst.*, p. 25: "Simplicius acquaints us that Empedocles made two worlds, the one intellectual and the other sensible; and the former of these to [be] the exemplar and archetype of the latter." [24]

211. In the night the beasts of prey range abroad to destroy and devour, but when the SUN rises, they lie down in their dens. So, in a dark time in the moral world, devils or roaring lions walk about, seeking whom he may devour, but when the sun of righteousness shall arise, he shall be confined to the bottomless pit. (Ps. 104.21, 22.)

212. The immense magnificence of the visible world in inconceivable vastness, the incomprehensible height of the heavens, etc., is but a type of the infinite magnificence, height, and glory of God's work in the spiritual world: the most incomprehensible expression of His power, wisdom, holiness and love in what is wrought and brought to pass in that world, and the exceeding greatness of the moral and natural good, the light, knowledge, holiness, and happiness which shall be communicated to it, and therefore to that magnificence of the world, height of heaven. Those things are often compared in such expressions: Thy mercy is great above the heavens, thy truth reacheth; thou hast for thy glory above the heavens, etc. (See Image 21.)

THE BEAUTY OF
THE WORLD

THE beauty of the world consists wholly of sweet mutual consents, either within itself or with the supreme being. As to the corporeal world, though there are many other sorts of consents, yet the sweetest and most charming beauty of it is its resemblance of spiritual beauties. The reason is that spiritual beauties are infinitely the greatest, and bodies being but the shadows of beings, they must be so much the more charming as they shadow forth spiritual beauties. This beauty is peculiar to natural things, it surpassing the art of man.

Thus there is the resemblance of a decent trust, dependence and acknowledgment in the planets continually moving round the sun, receiving his influences by which they are made happy, bright and beautiful: a decent attendance in the secondary planets, an image of majesty, power, glory, and beneficence in the sun in the midst of all, and so in terrestrial things, as I have shown in another place.

It is very probable that that wonderful suitableness of green for the grass and plants, the blues of the skie, the white of the clouds, the colours of flowers, consists in a complicated proportion that these colours make one with another, either in their magnitude of the rays, the number of vibrations that are caused in the atmosphere, or some other way. So there is a great suitableness between the objects of different senses, as between sounds, colours, and smells; as between colours of the woods and flowers and the smells and the singing of birds, which it is probable consist in a certain proportion of the vibrations that are made in the different organs. So there are innumerable other agreeablenesses of motions, figures, etc. The gentle motions of waves, of [the] lily, etc., as it is agreeable to other things that represent calmness, gentleness, and benevolence, etc. the fields and woods seem to rejoice, and how joyfull do the birds seem to be in it. How much a resemblance is there of every grace in the field covered with plants and flowers when the sun shines serenely and undisturbedly upon them, how a resemblance, I say, of every grace and beautifull disposition of mind, of an inferiour towards a superiour cause, preserver, benevolent benefactor, and a fountain of happiness.

How great a resemblance of a holy and virtuous soul is a calm, serene day. What an infinite number of such like beauties is there in that one thing, the light, and how complicated an harmony and proportion is it probable belongs to it.

There are beauties that are more palpable and explicable, and there are hidden and secret beauties. The former pleases, and we can tell why; we can explain the particular point for the agreement that renders the thing pleasing. Such are all artificial regularities; we can tell wherein the regularity lies that affects us. [The] latter sort are those beauties that delight us and we cannot tell why. Thus, we find ourselves pleased in beholding the colour of the violets, but we know not what secret regularity or harmony it is that creates that pleasure in our minds. These hidden beauties are commonly by far the greatest, because the more complex a beauty is, the more hidden is it. In this latter fact consists principally the beauty of the world, and very much in light and colours. Thus mere light is pleasing to the mind. If it be to the degree of effulgence, it is very sensible, and mankind have agreed in it: they all represent glory and extraordinary beauty by brightness. The reason of it is either that light or our organ of seeing is so contrived that an harmonious motion is excited in the animal spirits and propagated to the brain. That mixture we call white is a proportionate mixture that is harmonious, as Sir Isaac Newton [1] has shown, to each particular simple colour, and contains in it some harmony or other that is delightfull. And each sort of rays play a distinct tune to the soul, besides those lovely mixtures that are found in nature. Those beauties, how lovely is the green of the face of the earth in all manner of colours, in flowers, the colour of the skies, and lovely tinctures of the morning and evening.

Corollary: Hence the reason why almost all men, and those that seem to be very miserable, love life, because they cannot bear to lose sight of such a beautiful and lovely world. The ideas, that every moment whilst we live have a beauty that we take not distinct notice of, brings a pleasure that, when we come to the trial, we had rather live in much pain and misery than lose.

NOTES

INTRODUCTION

1. Edwards Manuscripts, XI, No. 6, Yale University Library.
2. Jeremy Taylor, *The Rule and Exercise of Holy Dying, Works,* ed. Reginald Heber, London, 1839, IV, 342.
3. Thomas Hooker, *The Soules Exaltation,* London, 1638, pp. 104–105.
4. *Pensées,* 672.
5. For characteristic treatment of types in early New England literature, see: John Cotton, *A Brief Exposition with Practical Observations upon the Whole Book of Canticles,* London, 1655. *A Brief Exposition with Practical Observations upon the Whole Book of Ecclesiastes,* London, 1654.
James Noyes, *The Temple Measured,* London, 1647.
6. Cf. Perry Miller, *The New England Mind,* New York, 1939, chaps. xi, xii.
7. John Flavel, *Husbandry Spiritualized,* London, 1669, pp. A3 recto–A4 recto. The book circulated widely in New England, and two editions were brought out at Boston, in 1709 (advertised as the "10th") and in 1725. Even so, the signers of the testimonies in Mather's *Agricola* say that in 1727 the book was not always available.
8. *Ibid.,* pp. 24–29.
9. Cotton Mather, *Diary, Collections,* Massachusetts Historical Society, Series VII, VIII, 223.
Cotton Mather's efforts at adapting the spiritualizing technique to America may be traced in the following works:
Wonderful Works of God Commemorated, Boston, 1690.
Brontologia Sacra: the Voice of the Glorious God in the Thunder, London, 1695.
Fair Weather, Boston, 1692.
Winter Meditations, Boston, 1693.
Christianus per Ignem, Boston, 1702.
The Religious Marriner, Boston, 1700.
The Sailours Companion and Counsellour, Boston, 1709.
The Fisher-mans Calling, Boston, 1711.
Winter Piety, Boston, 1712.
Present of Summer-fruit, Boston, 1713.
The Voice of God in a Tempest, Boston, 1723.
Agricola, or the Religious Husbandman: The main intentions of religion served in the business and language of husbandry, Boston, 1727.
10. *Christianus per Ignem,* pp. 11–12.
11. *Ibid.,* p. 166.
12. *Agricola,* "Recommendations."

13. *Ibid.*, p. 3.

14. *Ibid.*, p. 212.

15. *Christianus per Ignem*, p. 12.

16. *Miscellaneous Observations on Important Theological Subjects*, Edinburgh, 1793, p. 397.

17. The difference between Edwards' and Mather's mentality can be seen by comparing Edwards' use of gravity in an image (Image 79, p. 79) and Mather's "improvement" of the happy fact that Newton would not commit himself as to the cause of gravity:

"It must be religiously resolved into the immediate Will of our most wise Creator who, by appointing this Law throughout the material World, keeps all Bodies in their proper Places and Stations, which without it would soon fall to pieces, and be utterly destroy'd." *The Christian Philosopher*, London, 1721, p. 82.

18. Sereno Dwight, *The Life of President Edwards*, New York, 1830, p. 30.

19. *Ibid.*, p. 669.

20. *Ibid.*, p. 703.

21. *Ibid.*, p. 702.

There is no evidence that Edwards ever read Berkeley; his "Notes on the Mind" and "Notes on Science" are independent achievements. Edwards seized with avidity upon every work of European philosophy that came his way, and cited his authors with the same conscientiousness with which he mentions Locke, Ramsay, or Turnbull. Had he read Berkeley he would have acknowledged him. Much speculation has been wasted on the question of Berkeley's influence, generally by scholars who have not appreciated the nature of the Puritan scholarship in which Edwards was raised, the Ramist logic and technologia. If Edwards' "Notes" are seen as a product of this tradition radically modified by the impact of Locke and Newton, there is no need to suppose any Berkeleyan assistance. Consequently parallels between Edwards and Berkeley are the more arresting because they testify, not to an influence, but to certain tendencies of the age which Locke had set in motion. Sooner or later, given the intellectual situation, persons of one kind of temper were bound to find Locke leading or forcing them toward something that must be called idealism, although Locke had had no such intention. If Edwards or Berkeley are read as kindred spirits, the similarities in their responses become understandable. What must be equally stressed, and has not been sufficiently clarified, are the great differences, even when Edwards' phrases seem almost to echo Berkeley's.

With these considerations firmly in mind, we may invite comparison between the young Edwards' improvement upon Locke—that pure discourse must consist of "naked ideas"—and Berkeley's argument, in the preface to *A Treatise Concerning the Principles of Human Knowledge* (Dublin, 1710), that the abuse of words has hindered the advancement of philosophy because words impose upon the understanding, and that therefore, "whatever Ideas I consider, I shall endeavour to take them bare and naked into my view; keeping out of my thoughts, so far as I am able, those names which long and constant use hath so strictly united with them." Par. 21.

In Berkeley, this hostility to "words" and the effort to purge ideas from their contamination followed upon his fear that the Lockean psychology would confirm a habit, already nurtured for a century by the example of Descartes, of attributing to subjective ideas a reality of their own. In Edwards, this motive was entirely lacking. The Puritan tradition, the heritage of technologia, enabled him to assume, as a matter beyond question, that ideas could exist nowhere but in the mind of God. What for Berkeley was the major threat to Christian philosophy had not yet shown its face in provincial New England. The source of Edwards' hunger for naked ideas was as much rhetorical as metaphysical: it was a recrudescence of the old Puritan appetite for *verbum sine ornatu.*

22. *An Essay Concerning Human Understanding,* Bk. II, chap. ix, Par. 21.

The moral abstractions—piety, virtue, justice—which Flavel, Cotton Mather, and other practitioners of the art of spiritualizing tried to elicit from objects were what Locke called "mixed modes." Locke's analysis of how the understanding becomes acquainted with these ideas in experience shows how, the physiological machinery of perception being what he said it is, most men would naturally acquire only what Edwards called "confused appearances" out of things. From Locke, Edwards learned that the essence of the problem of thinking with clarity about mixed modes is a problem of language:

"But as for mixed modes, especially the most material of them, *moral words,* the sounds are usually learned first: and then, to know what complex ideas they stand for, they are either beholden to the explication of others, or (which happens for the most part) are left to their own observation and industry; which being little laid out in the search of the true and precise meaning of names, these moral words are in most men's mouths little more than bare sounds." Bk. III, chap. ix, Par. 8.

Edwards defined a mixed mode as an "idea composed according to the will and pleasure of men." The spiritualizers, left to their own meagre powers of observation, were expending no great industry in searching for "the true and precise meaning of names," with the result that their sketchy improvements of objects were little more than "bare sounds." What Edwards wanted was the innermost meaning stripped of all adventitious associations. For him, even more than for Locke, the principle of "association of ideas" was a danger; it was the seductress for which rhetoric was the pander.

23. Dwight, *Life,* p. 666.

24. *Works,* ed. Sereno Dwight, New York, 1830, II, 51.

25. "Miscellanies," No. 201, Edwards Manuscripts.

26. *Ibid.,* No. 260.

27. *Works,* III, 152–153. Cf.: "In every case where the object of knowledge is the very inwardness of the subjectivity of the individual, it is necessary for the knower to be in a corresponding condition." Kierkegaard, *Concluding Unscientific Postscript,* trans. Swenson and Lowrie, Princeton, 1944, p. 51.

28. *Works,* II, 19.

29. "Sermon on Acts 13.41," Edwards Manuscripts.

30. A study of the revival of typology in Protestant countries during the seventeenth century would, it seems to this editor, make a substantial contribu-

tion to an understanding of modern literature. Salomon Glassius' *Philologia Sacra*, first issued in 1623–36, was printed again at Leipzig in 1705. Other titles in the revival are:

Thomas Taylor, *Moses and Aaron, or the Types of the Old Testament Opened*, London, 1653.
Samuel Mather, *Old Testament Types Explained and Improved*, London, 1673.
K. Vitringa, *Observationes Sacra*, 3 vols., Franeker, 1689–1708.

A great stimulus for the renewed study of the types was also provided by the leading Dutch theologians of the century, Witsius and Cocceius; since these men were leaders of the "federal" or "covenant" school of Calvinism, to which the New Englanders belonged, they were much respected and read in America. There was an extravagant flowering of typology in Holland at the end of the century, in which the chief names are Cramer and Vitringa. It should also be noted that in the German Pietist movement of the eighteenth century, especially in the school of Wurtemberg, typology was much cultivated by such leaders as Bengel and Hiller. Edwards can be described, if one uses the word carefully, as the leader of an American "pietism"; the similarity between his interest in typology and that of the German revivalists, of whose existence he was ignorant, is striking.

31. Benjamin Keach (1640–1704), *Tropologia: A Key to Open Scripture Metaphors . . . Together with Types of the Old Testament*, London, 1681. This immense folio volume was reissued in 1769 with an array of testimonials from English nonconformist divines, showing how extensively in such circles it was appreciated. Keach's distinctions between metaphor and type are interesting as giving us the concepts with which Edwards started:

"Similitudes or Metaphors are borrowed from visible Things, to display and illustrate the excellent Nature of invisible Things. Yea, heavenly Things are often called by the very Names, that material or earthly Things are; which is not to obscure or hide the meaning of them from us, but to accommodate them to our Understandings." Ed. 1769, p. iii.

"I believe there is a great Difference between metaphorical and typical Scriptures. . . . 1. Types suppose the Verity of some History, as *Jonah's* being three Days and three Nights in the Whale's Belly. When it is applied to Christ in the New Testament, it supposeth such a Thing was once done. Allegories have no such Supposition, but are as Parables, propounded for some Mystical End. 2. Types look only to matter of Fact, and compare one Fact with another, as Christ's being Slain and lying three Days in the Grave, to Jonah's lying so long in the Whale's Belly. But Allegories take in Words, Sentences, and Doctrines, both of Faith and Manners. . . . 3. Types compare Persons and Facts under the Old Testaments, with Persons and Facts under the New, thus prefiguring another to come. Allegories regard Matters in Hand, and intend the explaining some mystical Sense upon the Word, which at present they do not seem to bear. 4. Types are only Historical, and the Truth of Fact agreeing in the Antitype, makes them up. But Allegories are not intended to clear Facts, but to explain Doctrines, affect the Heart, and convince Conscience. . . . Hence many learned and judicious Persons are of Opinion, that Allegories and Metaphors are more extensive and comprehensive in their Meaning, and Applications, than Types:

though Care ought to be had that they are not run beyond the Analogy of Faith," pp. iii–iv.

Keach's last sentence reflects the still lingering distrust of the early Puritans for typology, and the major part of his tome is devoted to the safer considerations of plain rhetoric. Yet his discussion of the types exhibits what, to a mind imbued with Newton, could become the grounds of a renewed interest, the fact that the types are something hidden and yet intelligible, just as gravity had been, which ultimately are *seen:*

"*A typical Sense is when Things hidden,* or unknown, *whether present, or to come,* especially when the Transactions recorded in the Old Testament prefigure the Transactions in the New, *are exprest by external Actions, or prophetical Vision,*" p. 228.

32. *Works,* IX, 44, 84.

33. Augustine, *Divine Providence and the Problem of Evil,* trans. Robert Russell, New York, 1942, p. 167.

34. *Pensées,* 648.

35. *Works,* IX, 110.

36. *Confessions,* V, 24.

37. "Miscellanies," No. 638 (cf. p. 52). If Edwards the poet found in the types an image of nature freed from the encumbrances of rhetoric, Edwards the philosopher found them of invaluable help in defining the concept of "intention" after the fashion he had learned from Locke's chapter on "Power" in the *Essay.* The human will necessarily acts according to its perception of the total situation, and what it is able to perceive is what it intends; Edwards extended this pattern into the cosmos: God therefore has certain foreknowledge of all events. If God has no intention, He must be reduced to "contrivances . . . to mend and patch up, as well as He can, His system, which originally was all very good, and perfectly beautiful; but was marred, broken and confounded by the free Will of angels and men." Irresponsible rhetoric thus becomes one with "Arminian" theology, but perception of the types is perception of the unalterable law of God, of the cosmic necessity. Cf. *Freedom of the Will,* Part II, Section xi.

38. *Works,* IX, 110–111.

39. Augustine, quoted in Note 2, *Confessions,* Everyman's Library, New York, 1946, p. 62.

40. *Institutes,* I, vii, 1.

41. *Ibid.,* I, v, 11, 15.

42. Dwight, *Life,* p. 702.

43. "Sermon on Luke 16.24," Edwards Manuscripts. Cf. Image 149.

44. "Sermon on 2 Corinthians 13.5," Edwards Manuscripts.

45. Edwards' definition of typology, and the distinction for which he labored between a type and a rhetorical construction appear in this passage:

"It is an argument that the historical events of the Old Testament in the whole series of them, from the beginning of God's great works for Israel in order to their redemption out of Egypt, even to their full possession of the promised land in the days of David, and the building of the temple in the days of Solomon, were typical things, and that under the whole history was hid, in a mystery or parable, a glorious system of divine truth concerning greater things than these, that a plain summary, rehearsal or narration of them is called a parable and dark saying or enigma. Psalm 78.2. It is evident that here by a parable is not meant merely a set discourse of things appertaining to divine wisdom, as the word parable is sometimes used; but properly a mystical, enigmatical speech signifying spiritual and divine things, and figurative and typical representations; because it is called both a parable and dark saying." *Works* IX, 28. Spiritual truth thus is "hidden" in the events; to talk about or around the truth is, like all ordinary speaking, to talk of things appertaining to the subject but not of the subject itself. So allegories, parables, and metaphors use materials appertaining to theology, but the type *is* theology, the dark saying for the elucidation of which it is legitimate, though hazardous, to use rhetoric.

46. "Miscellanies," No. 777.

47. "Sermon on Luke 24.32," dated June, 1736, Edwards Manuscripts.

48. "Miscellanies," No. 408.

49. *Ibid.*, No. 296.

50. Dwight, *Life*, p. 687.

51. "Miscellanies," No. 777.

52. Emerson, *Works*, Boston, 1903, I, 41. Harriet Beecher Stowe, brought up in the Edwardsean tradition, understood many of its implications better than the theologians who endeavored to follow him, and could evaluate his achievement in terms that are fundamental for understanding American culture:

"The ministers of the early colonial days of New England, though well-read, scholarly men, were more statesmen than theologians. Their minds ran upon the actual arrangements of society, which were in a great degree left in their hands, rather than on doctrinal and metaphysical subtilties. They took their confession of faith just as the great body of Protestant reformers left it, and acted upon it as a practical foundation, without much further discussion, until the time of President Edwards. He was the first man who began the disintegrating process of applying rationalistic methods to the accepted doctrines of religion, and he rationalized far more boldly and widely than any publishers of his biography ever dared to let the world know. He sawed the great dam and let out the whole waters of discussion over all New England, and that free discussion led to all the shades of opinion of our modern days. Little as he thought it, yet Waldo Emerson and Theodore Parker were the last results of the current set in motion by Jonathan Edwards." *Old Town Folks*, Boston, 1897, p. 229.

IMAGES OR SHADOWS OF DIVINE THINGS

1. Cf. Image 58, p. 63.

2. Edwards' "Notes on the Scriptures," in Yale University Library, consist of a small Bible, King James version, which has been interleaved into blank folio pages, and three volumes of numbered annotations. The Bible evidently belonged first to Benjamin Pierpont and has Edwards' autograph with the date 1748. Edwards made his shorter annotations on the folio pages; longer re-

flections were entered in the manuscript volumes and a reference to the number of the passage put opposite the biblical verse. The whole set is elaborately cross-indexed, and shows evidence of hard use.

3. "Miscellanies," No. 487, is a discussion of the incarnation, in the course of which substantially this passage occurs; Edwards evidently realized, after he had written the argument, that this bit constituted an "image."

4. Cf. "Miscellanies," No. 119: "The things of the Ceremonial law are not the only things whereby God designedly shadowed forth spiritual things; but with an eye to such a representation were all the transactions of the life of Christ ordered, and as much of the wisdom of God in the creation appears in His so ordering things natural that they livelily represent things divine and spiritual, as the sun, a fountain, a vine; as also much of the wisdom of God in His providence appears in that the state of mankind is so ordered that there are in-numerable things in human affairs that are lively pictures of the things of the Gospel, such as shield, tower, marriage, family."

5. Edwards' note on I Cor. 15.42 is substantially the same as this text. I have been unable to find in the surviving manuscripts any exposition of Cant. 2.11.

6. Ephraim Chambers, *Cyclopaedia, or an Universal Dictionary of Arts and Sciences,* London, 1728, II, 367, article "Jasper":

"The florid Jasper, found in the *Pyreneans,* is usually stained with various Colours, tho' there are some that have but one Colour, as Red or Green; but these are the least valuable. The most beautiful is that bordering on the Colour of Laque, or Purple, next to that the Carnation; but what is now usually taken is Green, spotted with Red."

7. No manuscript of this sermon appears to have survived.

8. "Notes on the Scriptures," No. 342, repeats the phraseology of this entry, and adds: "So in the first state of man in his infancy is an image of what man . . . is in himself, a poor, polluted, helpless worm."

9. "Notes on the Scriptures," Ps. 68, No. 319, is a long parallel between the bringing up of the Ark out of the house of Oed-edom into Jerusalem and the ascension of Christ; it is printed in *Works,* IX, 346–350. Considerable light is cast on Edwards' methods of work in composing the "Images" by the fact that this note refers to Mastricht and Chambers. Petrus Van Mastricht, *Theoretico-Practica Theologia,* Utrecht, 1625, was a work of reference for Protestant scholars which was used in New England education from the first days; on p. 597 is a comparison of the ascension of Christ to a Roman triumph. Edwards evidently followed this clue by looking up "Triumph" in Chambers, *Cyclo-paedia,* II, 254, where he found the description on which this image is based. Compare, for instance, Edwards' text with:

"He was richly clad, in a Purple Robe Embroider'd with Figures of Gold, setting forth his glorious Atchievements: His Buskins were beset with Pearl, and he wore a Crown, which at first was only Laurel, but afterwards, Gold."

Edwards perceived that he had here exactly what he meant by a type. He in-corporated a few details from Mastricht, and rearranged the sequence of items from Chambers for more dramatic effect. Chambers is a better illustration of the benevolent temper of the eighteenth century than Edwards: he finds the strangling of the captives "horrible amidst all this Mirth," but Edwards, thinking of the ritual as a type of the Judgment, takes the destruction of the reprobate without flinching.

10. This seems to be a grim reflection of Edwards' disillusion with the results of the Great Awakening: those who had been awakened by his preaching soon settled down to a smug satisfaction with their own righteousness, and the leaders of the community, full of "favour and esteem," conspired to expel him from his church. Edwards' efforts throughout the rest of the manuscript to find among the images the pattern of an "outpouring" of the spirit testify to the depth of the wound he suffered in that experience.

11. Mathew Henry (1662–1714), *Exposition of the Old and New Testament*, London, 1708–10, is a monumental piece of scholarship that still is a standard work of reference in libraries that stem from the Calvinist tradition. It owed its success in great part to its being the first commentary to incorporate the new science into Protestant orthodoxy. The tone is revealed in Henry's comment on Genesis 1.1: It is "easy to observe" in the visible world, 1. variety, 2. beauty, 3. exactness and accuracy ("To those that, with the help of microscopes, narrowly look into the works of nature, they appear more fine than any of the works of art"), 4. power ("It is not a lump of dead and inactive matter, but there is virtue, more or less, in every creature; the earth itself has a magnetic power"), 5. order ("A mutual dependence of being, an exact harmony of motions, and an admirable chain and connexion of causes"), 6. mystery ("There are phenomena in nature which cannot be solved, secrets which cannot be fathomed or accounted for"). Henry then moralizes:

"But from what we see of heaven and earth, we may easily enough infer the eternal power and Godhead of the great Creator, and may furnish ourselves with abundant matter for His praises. And let our make and place, as men, mind us of our duty, as Christians, which is always to keep heaven in our eye, and the earth under our feet."

12. Franciscus Turrettinus, *Institute Theologiae Elencticae*, Utrecht, 1721, 3 vols. An immense commentary, long a work of reference for Protestant divines; in II, 545–546, Turrettinus explains that the word "vocation" as used in the New Testament derives from the custom of summoning athletes to the Olympic games.

13. In the manuscript this paragraph has been crossed out.

14. Ovid, *Metamorphoses*, I, 84–86:

"pronaque cum spectent animalia cetera terram,
os homini sublime dedit caelumque videre
iussit et erectos ad sidera tollere vultus."

15. In "Notes on the Scriptures," No. 271, Edwards has a discussion of the moon as a type of the varying degrees of revelation made to the patriarchs and prophets:

"The Gospel light granted to the Old Testament church in its different successive ages was very much like the light of the moon in the several parts of the revolution it performs, which ends in its conjunction with the sun."

Thus, the calling of Abraham and the first institution of the church by Moses correspond to the beginnings of a revolution of the moon; Isaiah represents the fullness of the moon in Old Testament history. Thereafter, Edwards sees the spirit of prophecy waning "as the light of the moon ceases as she approaches her conjunction with the sun."

In this passage Edwards incorporates the moon into the setting of biblical history; in "Notes on the Scriptures," No. 315, he treats it as an image of the soul, of the incarnation, etc., but in this image he permits himself a poetic rendering of the moon simply as a natural object. Thus his mind moved from a theological or a typical interpretation to, at least momentarily, a naturalistic appreciation.

16. Thomas Manton, *A Practical Commentary, or an Exposition with Notes on the Epistle of James*, London, 1653, p. 535:

"Pleasures nourish the heart, and fatten it into a senseless stupidity. Nothing bringeth a dulness upon it more than they. *Plutarch* observeth of the *Ass*, which is of all creatures the *dullest*, that it hath the *fattest heart*: Thence that expression in Scripture, *Go make their hearts fat*; that is, gross and dull. There is a fish which they call Ovos, the Ass-fish, which hath its heart in its belly; a fit emblem of a sensual Epicure."

17. The remainder of this entry in "Notes on the Scriptures" is a long interpretation of history, from the creation to the Day of Judgment, as a series of revolutions or cycles, each with its satellite revolutions; as in many of the "Notes" and "Miscellanies," Edwards was hammering out the structure of his *History of Redemption*, with which, in his last years, he was obsessed. This passage is a good illustration of Edwards' brilliant perception that the Newtonian world-machine needed the supplement of a scientific order in history.

18. The omitted section of this passage is a long recital of all the peoples Jehovah has cut off: Sodom, Korah, the Amalekites, etc. It is an array of the most gory passages of the Old Testament; again, Edwards was working out the scheme for his *History of Redemption*.

19. John Spencer, Καινὰ καὶ παλαιά: *Things New and Old. Or, A Store-house of Similies, Sentences, Allegories, Apophthegms, Adagies, Apologues, Divine, Morall, Politicall, etc. With their severall Applications*, London, 1658.

The preface is by Thomas Fuller, dated January 10, 1657. The book is a folio of seventeenth-century "emblems." Each is headed by a moral; each episode begins with some fact, from natural history (or unnatural natural history) or history, and works back to the moral. The reflection is frequently remote from the starting point. The passages are definitely "witty"; the deliberate effect is of ingenuity and immense miscellaneous learning.

Out of the 679 pages, Edwards takes three examples from pp. 68–69. Did he happen to pick the book up some place where he could read only one opening? Did he find these paragraphs quoted in something he was reading? Did somebody quote them to him?

A more interesting question would be, did he appreciate the difference between these witty emblems and his own images? His handling of the crocodile indicates that he cast off the baroque play of Spencer's fancy for a more rigid simplicity; the metaphor of the clock is copied almost literally; in the passage on the mole Edwards took only the topic sentence and developed the image entirely on his own. I have found no evidence elsewhere in Edwards' manuscripts that he read Spencer; yet on the cover of this manuscript he wrote "See Spencers Similies and sentences," as though to tell himself to read further in it.

20. The reference is to James Hervey's *Meditations and Contemplations*, London, 1746, in the section entitled "Reflections on a Flower-Garden":

"There are, I perceive, who still attend the flowers; and in defiance of the sun, ply their work on every expanded blossom. The *bees* I mean; that nation of chemists, to whom nature has communicated the rare and valuable secret, of enriching themselves, without impoverishing others; who extract the most delicious syrup from every fragrant herb, without wounding its substance, or diminishing its odors. I take the more notice of these ingenious operators, because I would willingly make them my pattern. While the gay *butterfly* flutters her painted wings, and sips a little fantastic delight, only for the present moment; while the gloomy spider, worse than idly busied, is preparing his insidious nets for destruction, or sucking venom, even from the most wholesome plants, this frugal community are wisely employed in providing for futurity, and collecting a copious stock of the most balmy treasures. And O! might these meditations sink into my soul! Would the God, who suggested each heavenly thought, vouchsafe to convert it into an *established principle;* to determine all my inclinations, and regulate my whole conduct!"

Edwards' primary concern was the revival of living piety against what he called, with intentional irony, "this age of light and inquiry"; therefore he welcomed as allies whatever seemed living, passionate, or emotional. So he welcomed Whitefield, whose hysterical emotionalism was far removed from Edwards' intense self-control; so he read the novels of Richardson with admiration, and so he evidently read Hervey. The contrast between Hervey's oratory and the restraint of Edwards' images helps to show what a unique figure Edwards was in the midst of the eighteenth century.

21. These passages are taken substantially verbatim from George Turnbull, *The Principles of Moral Philosophy. An Enquiry into the Wise and Good Government of the Moral World*, London, 1740, 2 vols. (The title page of the second volume reads: *The Principles of Moral and Christian Philosophy.*)

Turnbull was one of the opponents singled out for attack in Edwards' *Freedom of the Will* as being "a great enemy to the doctrine of necessity." Yet he was a disciple of Newton and Locke, and still more of Shaftesbury and Hutcheson, so that Edwards could find in him many of the premises from which his own arguments commenced. Edwards frequently invoked passages from Turnbull in order to refute Turnbull's positions. He found in Turnbull (who obviously derived it from Hutcheson) an analysis of the idea of beauty in sensational terms, as based upon a natural delight in symmetry, similar to the analysis of "excellency" Edwards had devised in "Notes on the Mind." In this passage Edwards is picking out remarks in Turnbull that seem to fall in with his conception of language; actually Turnbull is simply retailing Locke's thesis that language originates in sensible ideas and is pleading for a less "jejune and insipid" method of studying it. The point Turnbull is making, in I, 50–57, from which Edwards takes the first quotation out of its context, is that truth must find its way to the heart through the imagination and therefore the imagination should be cultivated in modern education! The contrast between Turnbull's rational optimism and what Edwards makes the excerpted passages seem to say, in the context of this manuscript, tells much of the story of Edwards' desperate effort to divert the course of the eighteenth century from goals toward which, in Europe and even in America, it was hastening apace. Turnbull's comfortable conclusion is: "Man therefore is made for eternal progress in moral perfection proportionally to his care and diligence to improve it"; Edwards' opinion of man's potentialities was less sanguine.

22. This entry is taken bodily from Andrew Michael Ramsay, *The Philosophical Principles of Natural and Revealed Religion*, Glasgow, 1748, 2 vols., II, 11–12.

Ramsay offered a complete philosophy of life and religion "unfolded in a Geometrical order." The book is another of the progeny of John Locke. Edwards may have received a copy from one of his many Scottish correspondents; it fitted in with the rationalizing tendency of Scottish Presbyterianism and was popular in those circles, as later it was among the Scottish realists in America. Edwards would probably have relished its formidable defense of Christianity against Descartes, Spinoza, Malebranche (from all of whom it gives copious quotations), and more especially for its attack upon "the errors, sophisms, and uncertainties of the Spinozists, Deists, Pyrrhonists, Socinians, Freethinkers, and minute philosophers of all kinds." Ramsay modeled himself consciously upon Newton, each point being delivered in a "Postulate" and followed by a "Scholium." To Edwards, Ramsay must have looked like an approximation to that "Rational Account" he dreamed of writing; the later portions of his "Miscellanies" are filled with pages copied from Ramsay.

Ramsay contends, in the standard eighteenth-century fashion, that revelation never contradicts reason; he makes a generous concession to the Deists by foregoing all proof from prophecies or miracles; he endeavors to show "that supposing these books divine, the doctrine contained therein is the only religion which justifies the ways of eternal providence, renders the Deity amiable to his creatures, reconciles all his moral attributes, far from destroying them; and in fine that the Holy Scriptures contain the most sublime system of theology and philosophy concerning God and nature, the visible and invisible world, that has ever yet been discovered." Edwards was so charmed with the extensiveness of this project that he could overlook certain respects in which he did not, or could not, agree with Ramsay.

Ramsay's second volume is addressed to the assertion "that vestiges of all the principal doctrines of the Christian religion are to be found in the monuments, writings, or mythologies of all nations, ages, and religions; and that these vestiges are emanations of the primitive, antient, universal religion of mankind, transmitted from the beginning of the world by the Antidiluvians to the Post-diluvian patriarchs, and by them to their posterity that peopled the face of the earth." This thesis was particularly acceptable to Edwards when he was devoting himself to *The History of Redemption*. But Ramsay was speaking in the conventional vein of the century; the primitive religion which thus descended to all peoples is so vaguely defined that it is practically one with the Deists' light of nature. Edwards was striving, to the limits of his scholarship, to work out a much more concrete, a much more historical thesis, that the pagan philosophers received the substance of their ideas from actual contacts with Judea, and that the unassisted light of nature had done nothing but distort them.

Although Ramsay employed the method of Newton, he was not a "consistent Calvinist" in Edwards' sense of the term. He declared, "We are far from believing that the Predestinarians are Spinozists; tho' we shall show that their fundamental principles lead to Spinozism." Edwards probably knew nothing of Spinoza at first hand, and was content with such condemnations as Ramsay's; yet out of Ramsay Edwards had to pick and choose, for Ramsay argued against Edwards' conceptions of original sin and freedom of the will. Still, he did supply Edwards, in his American solitude, with descriptions of the systems of Descartes, Hobbes, and Spinoza, and from such sources Edwards learned what he had to contend with. Edwards' great works were probably written with a conception of the philosophical situation founded upon Ramsay.

Hence it is interesting to note that Ramsay summarizes the position of "Dr. Berkeley" as being a denial "that there can be any abstract universal ideas; because all objects of our perception are concrete or particular." When Edwards and Berkeley are linked together in modern accounts, the assumption is that their "idealism" is similar or the same; if, as is likely, Edwards knew no more of Berkeley than such a summary given in Ramsay, he would have wholly agreed in condemning Berkeley's denial of abstract universal ideas.

23. John Stapferus, *Institutiones Theologiae Polemicae Universae, Ordine Scientifica Dispositae*, Tiguri, 1752, 5 vols. Stapfer is an immense work of polemical divinity, illustrating how much on the defensive Protestant theology had been thrown by the middle of the century; it presents a vast array of arguments against "Atheismo, Deismo, Epicuraeismo, Ethnicismo, Naturalismo, Judaismo, Muhamedanismo, Socinianismo, Indifferentismo Religionum, Latitudinariis, Religio Prudentum, Papismo, Fanaticismo, Pelagianismo, Remonstrantibus, Mennonitis sive Anabaptistis."

24. Ralph Cudworth, *The True Intellectual System of the Universe*, London, 1678.

Image 208 comes from the section in which Cudworth is describing the Stoics, for whom Puritans always had a particular fondness; the other images come from Cudworth's vindication of Empedocles from the charge of atheism even while admitting that he was an atomist. This defense would be of interest to Edwards, who was very much an atomist (the key to his early "Notes" is his thesis that the atom is a mental concept), and he would be particularly delighted to find that an atomist had used the conception of an archetypal system to refute "material causes and fortuitous mechanism." Edwards could feel that in the mid-eighteenth century his task was very similar.

In the youthful "Notes on the Mind" Edwards cited a passage from Cudworth. The appearance of these quotations, late in this manuscript, suggests that Cudworth may have been an influence on Edwards throughout his life. Yet it seems that Edwards always used Cudworth, as here, for incidental confirmations. In the "Miscellanies" his quotations from Cudworth come all in one series of entries, so that possibly he may have read Cudworth as an undergraduate and not had a copy in his hands again until the time he made these extracts. It is not necessary to suppose that "Cambridge Platonism" supplied Edwards with his ideas, any more than it is necessary to suppose he borrowed them from Berkeley. The starting point for all Edwards' thinking was Puritan theology and John Locke, whom he both accepted and criticized. Cudworth may have assisted him with the criticism, but Edwards was too thorough an empiricist ever to become any sort of a "Platonist."

THE BEAUTY OF THE WORLD

1. Edwards here reveals to what extent the influence of Newton upon his thinking was exerted through the *Optics* as well as through the *Principia;* to him, as to many religious and poetic spirits of the time, the *Optics* was, if anything, the more impressive, and in Edwards' case, the innermost meaning of his mysticism can be understood only with the help of this volume. Cf. Marjorie Hope Nicolson, *Newton Demands the Muse*, Princeton, 1946.